WHERE WAS GOD AT 9:02 A.M.?

ROBIN JONES

with
Sandy Dengler

Photographs by
Charles H. Porter IV

A
JANET
THOMA
BOOK

THOMAS NELSON PUBLISHERS
Nashville • Atlanta • London • Vancouver

Published in Nashville, Tennessee, by Thomas Nelson, Inc., Publishers, and distributed in Canada by Word Communications, Ltd., Richmond, British Columbia.

The Bible version used in this publication is THE NEW KING JAMES VERSION. Copyright © 1979, 1980, 1982, 1990, Thomas Nelson, Inc., Publishers.

Cover photo: Hundreds of search and rescue crews attend a memorial service in front of the Alfred P. Murrah federal building in Oklahoma City on May 5, 1995. Photo courtesy AP/Wide World Photos.

Jones, Robin, 1955-
    Where was God at 9:02 a.m.? : miraculous stories of faith and love from Oklahoma City / Robin L. Jones with Sandy Dengler ; photographs by Charles H. Porter IV.
        p.   cm.
    ISBN 0-7852-7577-0
    1. Oklahoma City Federal Building Bombing, Oklahoma City, Okla., 1995—Religious aspects. 2. Victims of terrorism—Oklahoma—Oklahoma City—Interviews. I. Dengler, Sandy. II. Title.
HV6432.J65   1995
364.1'64—dc20   95-31358
                                                 CIP

Dedicated to all of the wonderful citizens of Oklahoma City.

CONTENTS

Contents

The Author

Robin Jones, as general manager of Bott Broadcasting's KQCV/KNTL Radio, began hearing stories about the Alfred P. Murrah bombing very nearly as soon as it happened. Friends and acquaintances related wonderful tales and anecdotes. She realized that their stories presented a side of the tragedy most people have never heard.

The Photographer

Charles H. Porter IV, a twenty-five-year-old banker in Oklahoma City, has lived in the Edmond area since 1988 and has been a strong member of a local church there. Chuck loves taking pictures for a hobby, and does some freelance photography on the side. He is the amateur photographer who took the famous picture of baby Baylee Almon in the firefighter's arms, which was seen around the world. Many of the other pictures Chuck took that day and throughout the next month are included in this book.

Chuck is married to his lovely wife of two years, Sherylynn.

Mark W. Brown, pastor to collegians and young adults at Bethany First Church of the Nazarene, has also served churches in Dallas, St. Louis, and Owego, New York, as well as in Oklahoma. He worked as a chaplain and counselor during the rescue and retrieval at the federal building and is engaged in a number of community activities. The father of four, he is happily married to Vickie.

Cindy Katterson, a "transplanted Okie," works for a group of physicians in Oklahoma City. She is a published freelance writer who enjoys story-telling, planning creative parties, and participating in her church's Singles' Ministry.

Amy Rollins and her husband, **Ralph,** are business entrepreneurs and own a property management company. Amy is also involved in creative marketing projects and serves as a general partner for Paradigm Marketing.

Anne Wilson is a realtor. She has worked as a story producer for *PM Magazine,* an associate producer for a Public Broadcasting Services special projects, financial director for the Bush presidential campaign, and special events coordinator during the Reagan presidential campaign.

Acknowledgments

God orchestrated the involvement of each integral component to make this book a reality—a manifestation of synergy. In the physical realm, it was the sum of each of the individual stories contributed that made this book possible. A special thanks to the contributors who interviewed the people whose lives were touched—Mark Brown, Cindy Katterson, Amy Rollins, and Anne Wilson. I also have immense appreciation for those who offered their stories and for the KQCV/KNTL staff, especially Kristy and Lesa, for their daily help. A heartfelt thanks to the talent and skill of Sandy Dengler and Janet Thoma.

In the spiritual realm, the orchestration of prayers from tens of thousands of individuals from around the world made Oklahoma City one of the most spiritually empowered cities in the days and weeks following the bomb.

Thanks to each of you for making the sum total of the parts greater than the whole. Our prayers will be with all those who were impacted by the events which unfolded at 9:02 A.M. on April 19, 1995.

SOME OF THE PERSONS WHOSE STORIES
are told here are black, some white, some His-
panic, some "other."

    We have made no distinction in our text be-
cause at that time, in that place, no one made any
such distinction whatsoever. Quite simply, no one
noticed. Hero and victim, bereaved and survivor—all worked and prayed and hugged and
mourned together. As the tragedy and the hero-
ism unfolded, race disappeared. In this book we
can do no less.

Part One:

Terror in the Heartland

What Happened

EVERYONE WOULD HAVE AGREED THE world was normal at 9:01 A.M. on that Wednesday morning. It wasn't Monday, when everything goes wrong. It wasn't Friday, when you're about at the end of your tether. Wednesdays are ordinary.

People scrambled to get themselves and their kids ready to meet the day, sent the older children to school, and took the younger ones to day care. Everyone headed out to work, just like usual. The mayor, city officials, and local pastors met for their annual prayer breakfast. By 8 A.M. or so, the world was spinning in its proper orbit, the wheels of civilization turning the way they ought to turn.

A few minutes before 9, a Ryder rental truck pulled up in front of one of the federal facilities downtown. Not unusual. The truck dock was right there by the General Service Administration

(GSA) office in the Alfred P. Murrah building on Fifth. They were always getting stuff.

Then came 9:02.

Over two tons of fertilizer and diesel fuel inside the Ryder truck detonated. The shock wave flared out and up, slamming the north face of the building with a thousand pounds of pressure per square inch. The wave splintered the dark glass windows and drove the shards like shrapnel through the interior. It lifted portions of seven of the nine floors—those above ground level—straight up off their columnar supports and broke the columns.

Time elapsed: .007 seconds.

Pulverized street paving, the dirt from a crater eight feet deep and up to thirty feet wide, building stone and cement, glass, parts of the rental truck and other vehicles, and black smoke from burning across the street boiled upward into clear blue sky.

No longer supported, the portions of the upper floors that had been lifted free ripped away. They dropped onto each other like a stack of dishes, leaving a horrendous semicircular concavity in what had once been a smooth glass wall. Debris from the facade and north wall fell onto the street. Parts of the tortured floors tumbled into the basement all askew.

Almost directly across the street, a restaurant was destroyed. Also close to ground zero, the Journal-Record building lost all its glass and its roof. Catercornered across the street, the exterior of the building housing the Oklahoma Water Resources Board crumbled and a section of its roof was torn away. Cracks turned up in a number of buildings, and several graceful old churches sustained major damage. Windows all over town shattered and a large number of buildings became at least temporarily uninhabitable.

Time elapsed: about 6 seconds.

Dirt and debris lofted high by the explosion rained down over the area. Engine parts from vehicles fell two blocks away.

Before a minute had passed, nearly all the destruction had been accomplished. From then on, a few loose chunks and pieces would continue to fall. Water from ruptured lines would pour into the building's basement until the valves were closed. Eerie silence would crowd out the thunder. The black smoke would die back as the burning cars were extinguished. The gray dust would gradually dissipate.

The real story was about to begin.

CHAPTER ONE

Penetrating Questions

ON WEDNESDAY, APRIL 19, SHERMAN Catalon arrived around 7:30 A.M. and parked in the A level of the Murrah building garage as he always did. On his schedule was a meeting at 8:30 in one of the offices on the north side with the building manager and two others. Sherman was the assistant building manager, responsible for maintaining the Alfred P. Murrah building and all the other federal buildings located in downtown Oklahoma City. They were meeting with the district court clerk to talk about some renovations to the courthouse across the street to the south.

"From the office where we met," Sherman remembers, "we could look out at the traffic on Fifth, the vehicles and the pedestrians. Traffic was moderate that morning. We were assuming that the majority of the people we saw entering the building were going to the Social Security office, which opened at 9.

"That particular meeting ended around 8:50 or 8:55. The next, a staff meeting, was scheduled for 9:30 in the big conference room down the way. I went back to my office, which was just behind the manager's office. One of my employees came by to get an evaluation form from me and left.

"I had my back turned to the north wall, standing next to my desk. I picked up my telephone receiver, hit the button, and pow! A noise like a gunshot went off next to my ear. The ceiling and light fixtures fell on top of me."

Buried under that pile of ceiling tiles and fixtures, he could hear a rumbling noise. It was pitch dark. He braced himself, pretty well certain that the floor above was going to come down on him, and just as certain that he was going to die. He begged God, "Please! Not now!"

Sherman assumed that only his own office had been affected. Directly above it was a mechanical room with a big air handler. He figured something up there must have blown.

"I struggled to free myself and crawl out before the room above caved down on me. Why wasn't anyone calling to me, asking me if I was all right? That worried me.

"The interior partitions were nothing more than dividers, and they had all collapsed. It took me awhile to make it across the debris and out.

"The north wall, the whole north wall of the building, was gone. Daylight and a lot of smoke. I stood and gawked, stunned. One of my coworkers, covered with blood and soot, was crying out names. I didn't see anyone besides her.

"I returned to the room we had just left and found the two coworkers, also covered with blood and debris. I told them to stay there while I got help. I crawled out the interior window of that room.

"I must have been struggling and floundering in the debris longer than I thought because here came firefighters entering the building. I directed them to the area where my two coworkers were lying and stumbled out to the street. I was shocked, or maybe in shock, or both."

Bloodied people wandered all over. Sherman was afraid to look at his arms because they burned so. What about his other coworkers? He found a few of them outside and learned that they had been in the break room and missed the worst of the blast.

"The shock subsided enough that I went back inside to help rescue the injured. Everyone was frantic; everyone was in shock. Rescue workers and others came swarming in to help people out. When I went up to the fifth floor to assist with a fellow who had a broken leg and arm, I was amazed. That place is usually bustling, with lots of tenants. He was the only one I saw there. All that was left was a small portion of intact floor, like a little island.

"I went back to our office to make certain rescuers had gotten my coworkers out. They had. Then that second bomb threat forced evacuation. We all found ourselves running away from the building."

He hurried toward St. Anthony's Hospital because it was closest and therefore most likely to receive the first victims. He wanted to locate the coworkers he had not yet found. On the way, some of the family members of people in his department hailed him, their eyes betraying their shock and terror.

Recalls Sherman, "They asked me if their family members were all right. I was able to tell those particular people, 'Yes!' " They hugged him and wept.

Parents were showing up now, frantically asking about their babies. Was their child still alive? Sherman could find nothing comforting to tell them. The Murrah day-care center was devastated.

Because he worked in the building manager's office, he knew all the tenants—all the agencies and employees, and especially the child-care center. He also knew the building inside out, the whole layout and who was where, every inch. He remained at the site throughout the rescue effort for that reason. He could provide far more information than any blueprint could.

"Where was God just then? I can tell you. One of those coworkers lingered on this side of the building after our meeting to talk to someone; had he returned immediately to his own cubicle, he would have been killed. The staff meeting at 9:30 was scheduled for the big conference room, situated close to the Social Security office where so many died. Had that meeting been slated for 9:00 instead, our entire staff would have been on that north side where the floor tore loose and pancaked, and got crushed by all those upper floors. None of us would have survived. I called out to God and He spared me. At no point did God abandon me. He was right there all along, every moment."

Several days after, a friend approached him in amazement. "A few glass cuts on your arms. I can't believe you weren't killed or seriously injured. If you didn't believe in religion, I bet you believe in it now."

When Simple Answers Won't Do

Sherman Catalon was spared. But 168 other persons were not. Eighteen of those were small children.

Sherman Catalon prayed and received. But over the next days, many prayed just as fervently for relatives still trapped in the rubble to no avail. Indeed, for days, Sherman himself and his fellow rescuers prayed to find survivors. The last living person was pulled free that first night. Several in hospitals lingered awhile and died, even as others, including several tiny children, recovered miraculously. What worked for Sherman did nothing for many others.

People who viewed the immediate aftermath of the bombing, with hundreds of workers pouring out of the Murrah building onto the street will swear that the greatest miracle of all is that so many survived. And of the hundreds in the immediate area outside the building, only five are known to have been lost.

Sherman would point to the many survivals where there ought to have been no survivors as well as his own story as reason enough that God was there. Hundreds of people—thousands— millions, perhaps, as the tragedy gripped the nation—could not partake of that confidence.

That leaves unanswered the question, "Where was God?" Why would He permit this atrocity? How could He allow the murder of infants? Some who had trusted their lives to Him died; others among the faithful suffered unspeakable loss; yet didn't He promise to take care of His own? Until Timothy McVeigh was arrested, many fingers pointed to the local community of Islam and labeled them all extremists. "Here is your culprit!" But they were not. They suffered too.

This book is, first and foremost, a paean and a tribute to the heroes of Oklahoma City, sung or unsung. There are thousands of them. We hope to give you an intimate insight into that day and the days that followed. No work of fiction, no matter how much pathos and joy it contains, can come close to the drama of Oklahoma City's reality.

The deaths are tragic. But so many of the survivals are miraculous, and nothing less. We hope as we tell these stories to provide some answers to the question with which we began: "Where was God at 9:02 A.M.?" The lives, actions, and voices of many of the heroes themselves claim to know.

Perhaps we can offer some insight also into the totally unrelated, though no less important, question, "Why did He let that happen?"

And we hope to provide something more immediate and useful. Every person reading this book will suffer traumatic loss sooner or later, if he or she has not already. Based upon the experiences chronicled in these stories of Oklahoma City, we can offer some practical suggestions for dealing with profound loss.

Where was God at 9:02 A.M.? Let's look to these people to tell us.

CHAPTER TWO

Where Was God at 9:02 A.M.?

AN ARMY RECRUITER IN SAN ANTONIO, Texas, and a person based in St. Louis, Missouri, were talking to Captain Laurence Martin in Oklahoma City via a three-way conference call when the Oklahoma connection suddenly went dead.

It was 9:02 A.M.

Captain Martin had just been blown out of his office into the next partitioned area. A thousand daggers of shattered window glass had been blown through the room too. They pierced his left side— eye, head, and arm especially—and severed an artery in his right wrist.

Stunned past thinking, he watched his life-blood spurt. Tourniquet. That's what he needed, a tourniquet. Two others, a major and a civilian, had been thrown into the same area. The major took over, binding his own tie around Captain Martin's wrist to stem the blood flow. The captain was losing a lot of blood from his face also; the major used his shirt to temporarily solve that problem. The three of them headed for safety.

The north portion of the fourth-floor office area was gone. They looked out at blue sky and the Journal-Record building across the street. Gray dust still floated on the disturbed air. There was nowhere to go but the south side. Fighting debris all the way, they reached the back stairwell and made it down to the street.

Hundreds of workers were streaming down those stairs. Coming up them, a salmon swimming against the current, Captain Henderson Baker was returning to check on his people, the personnel in Army Recruiting. Like Captain Martin, he had been working on the fourth floor. Unlike Martin, he had fallen clear out of the building and landed in the street below.

A number of the people who survived, like Captain Martin and Sherman Catalon, are devoutly religious. A number who died were devoutly religious. For example, Valerie Koelsch's day job might be with the Federal Employees Credit Union, but she was an ardent worker for her parish. She referred frequently to her three families: her natural family, her church family, and her family at the credit union. Valerie saw the great need for a strong young-adult ministry in the Roman Catholic church and had a passion to help develop one.[1] She was on the third floor attending a meeting with six others when the bomb exploded. She was among those killed.

Those who survived will swear God was with them. There is no reason to doubt it. God was right there in those first few minutes, when so-called chance took some and spared others. Let's look briefly at who else was there.

Those First Hellacious Minutes

Where was everybody at 9:01?

The first floor housed the Social Security office. Although most of the workers arrived around 8:00, it opened for public business at 9. That day, Raymond Johnson was volunteering his time and services. He was on loan, so to speak, from the National Indian Council on Aging. A number of customers, early birds, had already arrived, hoping to finish their business and get on with the day. Social Security would lose sixteen employees, twenty-four customers, and their volunteer, Raymond Johnson. Over sixty people normally work there. Nineteen people survived.

General Services Administration (GSA), also on the first floor, provides materials, supplies, vehicles, and some services for U.S. government agencies. For example, when some agency of the

Department of the Interior or the Forest Service needs extra cars for the busy season, it leases them from GSA. A truck bay abutted the GSA area. GSA did next to no business with private parties and had no civilian customers as such. GSA would lose two. Twelve people survived.

The building's underground parking garage extended out beyond the first floor. Several people dumped into that area would be rescued. Margaret Goodson, one of the Social Security employees who died, usually took a smoking break around 9:00 in the parking garage with a friend. The friend was occupied with a customer that morning, however, and didn't go out. It probably saved her.

Nearly all the second floor was devoted to the contract day-care center. An excellent facility, it provided care for infants as well as toddlers and preschoolers. Three weeks before, the prior manager's contract had expired and the new contract was awarded to a different manager. She replaced several teachers, and a number of parents abruptly pulled their children out of the center. On April 19, the center served *less than half the children that had been there a month before*. Fifteen children and three workers died. Had the bomb happened in March, there could have been over forty children in the center.

Most of the third floor was leased by the Federal Employees Credit Union. The FECU, about half the size of the Social Security office downstairs, served a number of customers, but much of its business could be completed by phone or fax. The CEO, Florence Rogers, called a meeting with seven others, Valerie Koelsch among them. Only Ms. Rogers survived the meeting.

The Defense and Investigative Service of the Department of Defense operated out of the northeast corner of the third floor. Five of the unit's twelve employees were in the office. All five died.

The Federal Highway Administration and the Army Recruiting office took up the bulk of the fourth floor. A nest of engineers, the FHA handled much of the planning associated with federal highways. Eleven of their twenty-six employees died. Fifteen lived.

The Army Recruiting office, also concerned with other public affairs, employed forty people, most of them civilians. Eleven of those forty were gone that Wednesday. One of the soldiers, Lola Renee Bolden, had just taken the elevator down to the first-floor parking garage. She stepped out of the elevator right into the blast. Of the twenty-nine in the building that morning, they lost seven. But twenty-two people lived.

The Veterans Administration, the Department of Agriculture, and the Customs Service shared the fifth floor. Although most of the Housing and Urban Development's offices took up the seventh and eighth floors, the office of their inspector general, Paul Broxterman, was tucked down on the fifth floor beside Agriculture. He died. So did seven of Agriculture's fifteen employees working out of that office. In fact, veterinarian Peggy Clark usually didn't come into the office. She did that day. She and everyone else in her division died. Her supervisor, who very narrowly escaped, lived.

Three of the Customs Service's six employees were in that day. Two of them died. The third, Priscilla Salyers, came within an ace of being lost. Their supervisor would have been there, had he not stopped by the doctor's office. Four employees lived.

Of the fourteen people who worked out of the Marine Corps office on the sixth floor, most were out of the office. Captain Randy Guzman, a transplanted Californian, was sitting at someone else's desk—a desk right up against the north windows.

Housing and Urban Development took the worst of it. In all, they lost thirty-five of their 125 employees, a quarter of their force. Eight, though, tucked away up in a ninth-floor conference room for a computer training session, survived. Had they been sitting at their desks as on a normal workday, they would have been doomed. Ninety survived.

The Drug Enforcement Agency (DEA) used offices on the seventh and ninth floors. One agent congratulated a secretary regarding her un-born child—she was showing her sonogram around—and ran to catch the elevator as another was getting off. The one who got on the elevator survived, protected by the elevator shaft. The man who got off died. So did the pregnant woman. They lost five in all.

Alcohol, Tobacco, and Firearms (ATF) were up on the ninth as well. Initial rumors suggested that they might be the target of the bombers. All the ATF employees escaped.

The Secret Service lost six of ten. One of their agents had been married six weeks. Her husband became her pallbearer. Another had recently trans-ferred out from Washington; this Oklahoma tour of duty was, he reasoned, safer and less hectic. Four Secret Service men lived.

Approximately four hundred people—men, women, and children—were in the Murrah build-ing that day. One hundred sixty-three died. Over 230 people lived.

Meanwhile, Elsewhere . . .

Across the street at an angle to the northwest, the building housing the Athenian Restaurant was leveled. Rescue workers were digging there just as frantically. Beside it, two people died when a corner of the building housing the Okla-homa Water Resources Board was ripped apart. The Journal-Record newspaper building across the street to the northwest still stood, but all its glass had been turned into a million swift, slashing blades. The blast rocked the YMCA nearby, ripping out beams and ductwork and injuring the children and caretakers in their day-care center. *Miraculously, although injuries abounded, no one died.*

Just around the corner, the historic First United Methodist Church sustained severe damage. And therein lies a tale.

Pastor Nick Harris was going to tape four Holy Ground radio broadcasts in the sanctuary, so he arrived an hour early, around 7 A.M., in order to review the material. Gus Alfonzo, his sound engineer, was going to be there at 8:30, and he was never late.

"At ten 'til 9, Gus called," remembers Pastor Harris. "He had forgotten the appointment. In the three-and-a-half years we'd been making these broadcasts, that never happened before. Never.

"So I shifted gears into what was supposed to become an ordinary day. I walked downstairs to the kitchen where our two cooks were preparing for our Wednesday night dinner. We bantered a couple of minutes and I walked back toward the stairs leading to my office. The church property manager hailed me as I passed her door. She asked me to look at plans for the ducting of the new air-conditioning system we were going to install in a few days.

"We were bent over the blueprints when the floor shifted south and snapped back north. I heard the explosion, glass breaking, wood shattering. It took a moment to determine that the explosion had come from outside. We rushed out. The church is less than half a block from the site; we were among the first there. Emergency workers—police, fire—arrived in moments to take over the rescue operation at the federal building, so I turned my attentions to the children in the YMCA day-care center, across the street from the Murrah building.

"Where was God at 9:02? Let me tell you. Our sanctuary was instantly reduced to a horrible jumble of broken glass. Our wonderful stained-glass windows had been turned into thousands of projectiles. Bricks and wood lay everywhere. *Big* wood. Beams. Had my sound engineer and I been at our usual places recording those broadcasts, the skylight would have dropped on me. Gus would have had steel beams in his lap—or through his head. We would have been, at the very least, severely injured. I'm not stretching the point a bit to say we could have died.

"I did not deserve to be miraculously saved from death any more than I deserve to be saved from damnation. Only God's grace accounts for both."

Others Who Miraculously Survived

A block south of Alfred P. Murrah in the old post office building, Randy Swanson, the press secretary for Congressman Frank Lucas, was talking on the phone at 9:02 with his pregnant wife, Carol.

"The post office building seemed to explode," Randy remembers. "I don't know if I was literally blown over by the impact of the bomb or if I just jumped out of my chair. The next thing I knew I was on the other side of my desk. I ran out into the hall. Amy, our receptionist, was very emotional and the office was a mess. Light fixtures had fallen and insulation was dripping down out of the ceiling.

"I yelled, 'Get out of here! Get out of here!'

"There were only three of us there that day—Amy, Mary Kay, and myself. Everyone's windows were blown out, there was debris everywhere—but no Mary Kay. The two of us started rummaging through the debris; Mary Kay was stuffed down under her desk, shaking. We all ran out and down the hall to the front door.

"When we reached the exit, the doors were gone. Across the street, dozens of windows were broken out of the Bank of Oklahoma building, all the way to the top floor. It's over fifteen stories tall.

"Several minutes later we bumped into a co-worker, Derek, in the alley north of the building. He had run to my window and yelled for me. 'Swanson!' He shouted to a person he didn't even know, 'I can't find Swanson!'"

Carol Swanson heard those words, and they increased her anxiety. In fact she had heard everything that was happening.

"I heard glass shattering," she remembers. "I heard Randy shout, 'Get out!' so I kind of felt he was safe, since he could still yell. Over the line I heard people screaming. Then, not fifteen seconds later, the sirens in the distance.

"I could see the clock on the microwave changing numbers.

"Very faintly, I could hear someone calling for Swanson. I heard the voice shout, 'I can't find Swanson!'

"I called our seven-year-old, David, over and put the phone to his ear. 'Something really bad has happened,' I said, 'and we need to pray for Daddy right now.' So the two of us right there stopped everything to pray for him.

"Eight minutes on the microwave clock, and I kept that phone to my ear. Randy seemed safe when he dropped the receiver, but what if he ran into danger? And why couldn't that voice find him?

"Then call waiting beeped, and Randy was back on the line to tell me he was okay. When I hung up, we turned on the TV and realized the reality of the devastation.

"I wasn't certain what to do next, but I had an appointment with the obstetrician—that's why David was home from first grade; he wanted to go along—so I decided to go ahead with it.

"Later, a local news reporter interviewed David. At one point, the camera closed in on him for a close-up and he said, 'My mom and I know what a second means now.'

"The reporter asked, 'What do you mean by that?'

"'When the bomb went off, my daddy could have died in a second.'"

The media immediately picked up the phrase. "Now we all know what a second is."

The Swansons and Pastor Nick Harris felt God's presence at 9:02 A.M. So did Barbara Martin, wife of Captain Laurence Martin. When the windows rattled in their home, she turned on the TV. The station said the courthouse had been bombed.

"I prayed they were right and that it wasn't Laurence's building," Barbara remembers. "Then the news helicopter got some clear shots from an overflight. God had not answered my prayer.

"I ran across the street to a neighbor's, crying. So much for military composure. I was sure he was dead. My neighbor, bless her, came back to my house with me, and we watched the news report—the same one the rest of the world was seeing—and waited for word.

"About 10 A.M., I got a call from Presbyterian Hospital. Laurence was alive and they had to operate right away to repair his right hand and wrist. It turns out, he had been the second one admitted out of seventy-seven at that particular facility. Anyway, when I got there, I couldn't find him at first. A volunteer helped me. Thank God for the volunteers!

"My prayer that it be one building instead of another one was silly. I know that. It was the first thing I thought of. God, of course, is infinitely better than that. He was gracious enough to ignore the silliness and stay close to us in far more important ways, giving us what we *really* required. He provided Laurence what he needed—life and medical attention—and me what I needed. The comfort of an understanding friend."

Laurence Martin miraculously survived. So may have thousands of others.

And Maybe Even Thousands of Others

Theorists looking at the bomb and its effects have been tossing about some ideas that count as grace on a grand scale.

The bomb was not just a glorified, industrial-strength firecracker. Certainly, it was big, horribly big. The rear axle of the truck in which it was detonated fell upon a car parked a block and a half away, totaling it. Firefighters had to use a jaws-of-life to get a baby out of the backseat. One of the truck's tires landed on the roof of the Regency Towers apartments, twenty-four stories high.

Size, though, wasn't the most of it. The bomb performed its evil in fairly sophisticated ways. The impact and pressure waves it generated did not simply fly willy-nilly. And because of its complex pressure waves, all sorts of "what ifs" have been circulating.

What if the day had started out cloudy or rainy instead of sunny? Some pyrotechnicians believe that a low cloud ceiling would have deflected those waves that flew upward and sent them bouncing down to the ground again. Instead of the destruction we saw, the devastation would have destroyed much larger areas.

Grace.

The tale is also circulating that the driver of the Ryder truck intended originally to park on the south side of the federal building but could not find a space. Perhaps not fully realizing what the bomb did and how it did it—that is, not understanding the consequences of choosing one parking place over another—the driver ended up against the building's north wall.

Consequences? To explain in oversimplified terms, the expanding pressure waves from the explosion more or less assumed a cone form, widening as it rose. This is why more of the roof and upper floors of the Murrah building were blasted away than were the lower floors, which were actually closer to the bomb. On the north side of the street, it seems that the cone tended to rise and expand above the shorter buildings. The Journal-Record building's roof blew off; the low, open parking garage beside it suffered much less impressive damage. Part of the cone dissipated out beyond the parking lot where all those cars caught fire.

Had the truck been parked on the south side, that cone would have been deflected in different ways, far more destructive ways. The configuration of the buildings would have multiplied the wave effect. It would have taken out the Murrah building, the federal buildings to the south, and quite possibly most of the surrounding buildings. Many blocks of the city. The First United Methodist church would have been flattened instead of damaged, as would scores of other structures.

Grace.

Who's Right?

A second. Seven-thousandths of a second. The Sunday following, several pastors in the area preached that God had turned His back at 9:02— that a loving God would never have countenanced such an atrocity. In the same Sunday hour, other pastors preached that God's ways are inscrutable, but He promised He would never leave us or forsake us, and we can depend on that. Who's right?

Where was God when injustice ran roughshod? The question has been debated for millennia, and it will not be satisfactorily answered here. But the tragedy of the bombing in Oklahoma City provides some interesting and helpful observations, fodder for discussion. We can offer a possibility if not a definitive response.

God is generally associated with miracles, and miracles by the usual definition abounded that morning. The collapsing wreckage carried Priscilla Salyers from the fifth floor to the pile of rubble at the bottom. She emerged comparatively unscathed and a month later stood among those watching the implosion and razing of the building's ruined shell. People who were there agree that's miraculous. Where 163 died inside the building, hundreds escaped, most with minor injuries. People who were there say *that's* miraculous.

Brandy Ligons was not only pulled alive from the wreckage, a doctor just happened to attend her from the moment she was found and kept her asthma at bay. By the time she was extricated, medics with a device called a bag valve mask were delivering oxygen and assisting her breathing for her. People involved say her survival was miraculous.

With our new scientific awareness, modern men and women tend to discount miracles or explain them away. Indeed, we're most often taught to reject them entirely. There are, many claim, naturalistic explanations for whatever one might call a miracle. One of those explanations is chance. Random happenstance.

In a building with probably four hundred persons in it, say the doubters, numbers of them will escape death by being in the right place at the right time. For instance, those HUD people in the computer training workshop on the south side would have died had they been sitting where they usually sat on the north side. By chance, some, such as a young man delivering food to the daycare center and the USDA veterinarian who normally would not have been there, stepped into the jaws of death. A woman who happened to be using the bathroom attributes her survival to that extra wall. The woman who left the protection of the elevator might have survived, had she been a few minutes slower about coming down to the garage. But then, had the UPS driver who delivered some parcels to the Murrah building been slower, he would have died in the pancaked floors. He missed death by moments. Mere moments. Chance is a fickle manipulator.

Chance is the only explanation, they claim, for the fact that devoutly religious people lived even as others, equally devout, died. The survivors of the Murrah tragedy say, "You weren't there. You can't begin to realize what it was like in there. That building was a little piece of hell. One of the most impressive evidences of the presence of God is the occurrence of miracles, and it's a miracle I'm still here—that anyone is here."

Said Augustine: "Miracles lead us to faith and are mainly wrought for unbelievers."

And what a sign to those who didn't believe in God! They stood in awe of the unique spiritual nature of the tragedy. As clear and typical an expression of that nature as any was this sentence in the *Daily Oklahoman* editorial the next day: "Beyond intercessory prayer, here are things you can do to help neighbors in need."[2]

The call to prayer came first. Then came a recital of the organizations in the vanguard of the response—Red Cross, Oklahoma Blood Institute, Salvation Army. With phone numbers. Prayer plus practical response. Don't just pray. Do. Don't just do. Pray.

Over the days and weeks, the word *prayer* would turn up hundreds and hundreds of times in headlines and articles, not just in Oklahoma City but around the world. So would specific references to God, made by both ardent Christians and casual church and synagogue members of many stripes who found themselves suddenly paying more attention to spiritual matters. Many call that a "testimony."

Having no physical body (the fancy technical term is incorporeal), God by nature is invisible. You can detect His presence in two ways, neither of them subject to measurement: through His spirit felt within a person and among people, and through external indications of His influence in a situation.

Hundreds and hundreds of persons, whether they were directly involved in the bombing or not, testify to His presence within them at that time. Ask Sherman Catalon, Carol Swanson, the Martins, and many, many others. He was there, they'll tell you.

A powerful spiritual presence pervaded the whole incident, from 9:02 A.M. to the present moment. People all over the world comment on it. Even agnostics admit something unique happened; those who believe in God are certain what it was. The movement of what Christians call the Holy Spirit. In a word, God among us.

Others point to the miracles. Some say such surprising turns of events should be expected in a random world. Still others reply, but not *that* many. Altered circumstances are altered circumstances. You can doubt them, but they occurred in quantity. In fact, as we shall see, all manner of both sorts of miracles occurred.

God's felt presence and God's observed influence. That leaves begging two questions, "Why did this happen?" and "Why did some live and others die?" Those questions require more exploration and we'll explore them throughout this book. But right now, we can answer the one with which we began.

Where was God at 9:02 A.M.?

At the Alfred P. Murrah federal building in Oklahoma City. Before the week was out, Oklahoma's cry turned from "Terror in the Heartland" to "Together in the Heartland."

Here, out of the hundreds of stories to emerge from the death and destruction, we offer these true accounts of the miracles in the ashes:

- The Miracle of an Expert Response
- The Miracle of the Supernatural
- The Miracle of Ordinary People Doing the Extraordinary
- The Miracle of Comfort to Servants on the Edge
- The Miracle of Unity Despite Differences

Let us share these miracles with you.

Part Two:

Together in the Heartland

CHAPTER THREE

The Miracle of an Expert Response

WHAT WAS THAT FAMOUS LINE ON THE old *A Team* television series? "I love it when a plan comes together." As often as not, George Peppard uttered it at the close of some episode in which anything that could possibly go wrong with the team's plan had done so. In spades.

And yet in Oklahoma City emergency plans came together in ways no one could have imagined. Take the fire department, for instance.

There are a number of ways in which fire departments respond to emergencies. One is strictly random. When the call goes out, whoever is available responds with whatever apparatus happens to be handy at whichever station is closest. It's not a bad way to function in a limited setting, and small, rural, volunteer departments can't do much more.

The system used by the Oklahoma City Fire Department is several orders of magnitude better than that. In essence, the emergency response starts out small and expands when the need is greater.

Firefighters literally live to respond; they love it, and with this system, people who might want to go end up standing around idle. Too, there is a set of rules to follow. Protocols aren't usually much fun. A lot of rank-and-file firefighters were not real thrilled with the system of rules.

Fire Chief Gary Marrs put this advanced response system in place and then insisted that his firefighters use it on every call. Small calls provided oft-repeated practice for larger ones. He wanted everyone to be thoroughly familiar with the system's chain of command and methods of organization. He wanted everyone to be accustomed to making the level of decisions the system demanded, and quickly. If a major fire broke out, his department was ready. If a big twister ripped through the heart of Oklahoma City or its suburbs, his department was ready.

No one imagined a bombing.

General alarms—that is, every station in the city responding—are unheard of in Oklahoma City. Still, when the Big One came at 9:02 A.M., the system kicked in automatically. The general alarm went out. Everyone knew what to do; everyone made appropriate decisions. Chief Gary Marrs's plan came together better than anyone could have imagined.

It is understandable that when a major media reporter asked the assistant chief, in essence, "Can your department handle something this big?" the implications of that question offended a lot of people in Oklahoma. When the bomb exploded, Gary Marrs was seated at the helm of one of the best departments in the country.

Certainly, the chief dropped by the site frequently during the course of recovery. If his people needed something, he saw that they got it. But freed of the necessity to supervise directly, Chief Marrs was able to spend the bulk of his time meshing his people's efforts with those of the many other agencies on the scene—ATF (Alcohol, Tobacco, and Firearms), FBI, and all. The whole incident was handled smoothly in a coordinated way. The organization not only held together well but improved as days stretched into weeks.

Eventually, only two or possibly three victims still lay within the pile of rubble which supported a blasted wall. Workers marked that spot with a spray of international orange glow-paint. For the moment, they could safely dig no farther.

At 11:58 P.M. on Thursday, May 4, Chief Marrs placed a chair in the flat, cleared area that once had been the Social Security office and stepped up onto it. Jon Hansen, his assistant chief, stepped up onto another, as did Ted Wilson, the department's chaplain. Hundreds of workers, the last shift, gathered silently around. The three men, each in turn, expressed their profound gratitude to all the workers who labored at the disaster site. In-state and out-of-state. City agencies and state and federal agencies. The thousands of "ordinary" citizens, not ordinary by any stretch of the imagination, who volunteered time, efforts, service, money, and prayer. Jon Hansen then asked Ted Wilson to offer a closing prayer.

For the moment, at least, it was over.

Be Prepared

The sophisticated response system was not the department's only preparation. Like most fire departments, Oklahoma City conducted mass disaster drills now and then.

"You don't do it often," a firefighter explained. He was grinning, delighting in the recollection. "It ties up equipment you might need somewhere else if a genuine incident occurs, and it's expensive as all get out. Basically, what you do is set up a simulated disaster. A biggie. Let's say you start with a tornado that collapses a house and causes a bus wreck, add a multi-vehicle accident to it— junked cars spread around, you know—with a fire in a diesel tanker truck and an overturned cattle truck and five different people with heart attacks going on all at once.

"When it's all set up, dispatch tones us out. The appropriate units are supposed to respond—fire, emergency medical services, you know—and do the things they would do if the disaster were real. It's playacting with a purpose and it's a lot of fun." The grin faded. "The City ran a disaster drill like that less than a year before the Big One. We were ready."

The fire department and EMS were not the only agencies who prepared. Each spring during tornado season, the local chapter of the American Red Cross runs disaster drills in order to sharpen up the effectiveness of its workers. This time was not a test.

Expert Medical Response

Individual medical services and facilities prepare their own disaster plans. A splendid case in point, one of the many, is St. Anthony's Hospital, the facility closest to the site. Like others, they spent a lot of time developing a "what if" plan. "What if our facilities were crippled?" "What if two hundred people were dumped onto us all at once?" "What if . . . ?"

St. Anthony's would end up treating 173.

"It sounds fairly simple," explained a doctor there. "You have doctors, nurses, and techs on call and trained, ready to go at any time. When the alert goes out, they divide into two groups. One group takes care of patients already in the hospital. Nobody wants to be in that group, but of course it's just as important as the other. The other group meets the emergency. We also postpone elective procedures to free up personnel.

"It's not simple. The logistics involved are humongous, and our office staff are just great. You have to summon the right people and get them and equipment to the right places. Plans like that look good on paper, but you never know how it will do in a blood-and-guts mass emergency."

At 9:05 A.M., three minutes after the blast, St. Anthony's disaster plan had been activated.

"The first of the injured began arriving at 9:15. They were walking in and being driven in by total strangers. And, of course, the ambulances and aid vans. Paramedics on the aid vans said they had to lock the doors when they got out or scores of people would try to squeeze themselves into the rig.

"Some of the wounded suffered superficial problems. Others had life-threatening injuries. Our disaster plan worked so great, we took care of every single person like he or she was the Queen of England."

The doctor paused, then purred, "It was beautiful."

Lori Hansen-Lane, a facial cosmetic plastic surgeon, agrees. She was among those who responded quickly to the call for medical people. "Five or ten minutes after I arrived at St. Anthony's, they requested a plastic surgeon. A girl's ear had been chopped to the bone in two places. The cartilaginous support structure was a mess. She also had a bad facial laceration. I immediately started trimming edges and sewing on her. The quicker you get onto something like that, the better the outcome—the less tissue damage and scarring. I followed up on her, incidentally, and she healed beautifully.

"The next patients I attended that day were less serious. Bad cuts but not structural damage. St. Anthony's triage is excellent.

"You know, it's interesting how all the red tape went right out the window. No forms. No insurance. No delays. We just worked at what we did best. It was wonderful. If that isn't grace. . . ."

And then there was Doctor Bob.

The Expert Who Just Happened to Be There

Dr. Robert Bomengen, honored by the American Academy of Family Physicians as the American Family Physician of 1994, just happened to be in town. He was scheduled to lecture medical students at the Oklahoma University Health and Science Center.

"I never made it to the lecture," he says.

"I always carry my tools. I keep my bag stocked and take it with me wherever I go. You may be the best mechanic in the world, but if you don't have a wrench you cannot turn a nut. That's what I'm telling the kids. My bag has saved twenty-five lives, hands down."

April 19, Dr. Bob had his bag.

He took it with him to the closest emergency room. Doctors were scurrying everywhere. Dr. Bob figured this place had doctors aplenty; they were probably in short supply at the site. He needed wheels.

"I arrived on God's wings," he claims. "God provided an ambulance to escort me straight to the disaster site. What better way to get around police barricades than in an emergency vehicle?

"When I arrived at the site I saw a number of utility workers scampering down into manholes to help. Now those people were the real heroes in OKC that day."

With the supplies in his bag he bound wounds, helping out at the triage sites. He spent hours tending the wounded, until the glut of injured eased and all were transported.

"I saw a woman named Sadie curled up in a fetal position in the arms of a coworker. She was yelling and screaming and holding her abdomen. I bent over her and calmly said, 'My name is Dr. Bob. May I pray for you?' She calmed down until they loaded her into an ambulance. They tell me she lived.

"I never have had a patient of mine near death who has died without prayer. I always ask permission and I've never been turned down. My faith is important to me. I don't proselytize. I communicate my faith by example.

"I tell medical students there are nine tenets of my oath to success. One of the nine is faith. I try to emphasize a kindred spirit and a good heart. Medicine has been turned into a business and I don't like that. To me, medicine is a ministry.

"I often recount the events which led me to that place at that time, how everything came together so beautifully. The lecture had been arranged five months in advance. And look. My message has been magnified a thousand times by the tragedy in Oklahoma City."

Mechanics of Success

Personnel at St. Anthony's point to several aspects of the disaster plan which they believe profoundly enhanced success. For one, every victim immediately received the services of doctors and nurses who stayed with that patient clear through the course of treatment, from the greeting at the door through recovery. Not a single one got lost in the confusion; no one slipped through some crack.

Most important, the hospital staff on the floor made the decisions. No arbitrary choices came down from on high. The decisions were made based on experience, common sense, and the circumstances of the moment. When those decisions were critiqued after the fact, they proved to have been brilliant.

Were other facilities' disaster plans just as effective? Absolutely. Four hundred and ninety people from the explosion received hospital attention at fifteen facilities. *You can count on one hand the number of them who subsequently died.*

And large numbers of people injured by the blast never reported to hospitals so as to enter the statistics. Some treated their glass cuts themselves. Unwilling to add to the load thrust upon the hospitals, others went directly to their own doctors. The number of actual injured topped 600 and is still climbing.

The *Daily Oklahoman* put out a call to all those not formally treated. Researchers want to assay the effects of the bomb on the full population, not just those attended by medical facilities. They need a complete picture, and medical records offer only a limited one. That means getting stories and other information from the hidden victims, the ones the statisticians don't know about.

Why would they want that information?

Preparation, in case another big one occurs.

The Trained Teams

Not even a big city department can sustain a major operation for weeks on end without help. Life goes on, and the personnel and equipment must respond to all the community's needs of the everyday—fires, accidents, medical emergencies. At several places in the country, search and rescue departments have been built to mobilize instantly and go where needed. They can fill in behind the initial response, providing a continuation of professional support.

One such department is Pierce-King County Search and Rescue, who came to Oklahoma City about a week later. One of their rescue workers smiled. "The incident commander was briefing us when we got there. He said, 'I hope you guys don't mind a little rain.'

"'Rain? What's rain?' we said. 'We're from western Washington, the Seattle-Tacoma area. We get rain for days at a time. Weeks! Man, we *train* in rain."

Teams such as this train thoroughly and practice regularly. Ideally, of course, they would never be needed. Life is not ideal. They were needed in Oklahoma City.

In news footage and photos, you've seen the furry members: dogs trained to sniff out bodies and find any victims still alive. Too, technicians use electronic sensors to detect and hone in on the tiniest of movements within rubble—feeble tapping or scraping. Their infrared sensors can find minute differences in warmth. Living victims produce heat, as do you and I. Even bodies can be found.

The rescue division extricates both survivors and corpses.

"We keep up practice with the tools," explains the fellow from Washington state. "You need some weird stuff to get around obstacles or work through them. We can cut, jimmy, tunnel, and pry like you wouldn't believe. You've seen jaws-of-life on TV '911' shows. We use those. Sometimes it's the ordinary stuff that saves the day. Some of our guys teach courses on how to extricate somebody using nothing but a crowbar and a couple of cement blocks.

"Extrication is a science. We have to take so many hours of continuing ed every year just in extrication. The trick is to cause no further injury. There's no law that says we have to, but if we have the luxury of time—I mean if there are no living who need our services quickly—we treat the dead with the same respect we treat the living. You bag the corpses, but you want to do it reverently, you know.

"The people who are alive you strap down to a stiff board. When somebody talks about packaging somebody, that's what they're talking about. Immobilizing the patient so no further injury will occur."

The medical division accompanying the unit includes emergency medical technicians (EMTs), paramedics, and even surgeons at times. They stabilize the victims until they can be extricated, and usually continue care afterward.

"The people you don't see," the rescuer explained, "are our technical division. You should see what those guys can do with the really heavy rigging. They do our hazardous materials work. What we really love 'em for, though, is taking care of communication, housing, and meals. They handle the logistics of the operation. They also take care of our tools. Repairing them. Sharpening them. You can go through stone drills in a hurry."

The technical support people also keep the scrapbooks, so to speak, documenting the team's work on site with written reports, essays, and pictures. If you want information about the team, you talk to the tech.

The Task Force Leader braids all these strands together into a tough, effective unit. As a side result, he or she can pick out in a flash the strengths and weaknesses of a search and rescue unit.

Jim Strickland, Task Force commander of the Fairfax County (Virginia) Search and Rescue Department, instantly saw the strength of the New York City Search and Rescue Unit. They asked for and received extra time to work on site. Then, says Strickland, "At 8 A.M., the day the New York team left, they stopped by the north side of the Murrah federal building and had a group prayer. That really touched me."

Team Members

The initial rescue effort used anyone who showed up. The object was to reach survivors quickly and to that end, volunteers crawled over dead bodies and dismembered parts to dig out the living. It was a heady, hideous, engrossing few hours. Rescue efforts then settled into a more deliberate, organized, methodical search using uniformed personnel primarily.

Photos and video footage of the rescue effort that you might have been watching show a lot of usually colorful jumpsuits and turnouts (pants with suspenders and coat, made out of heavy treated canvas) crawling around the ruins. Even dull clothing stood out against the harsh, cold gray of the rubble. These were the trained responders, prepared to step forward in an emergency of this sort.

One of the first rescuers to dig into the basement rubble still can't sleep well at night. "During those first hours when we were still extricating live ones, I was crawling around in the basement. Blood was just raining down through the broken cement and beams. We know now, of course, that it was from the people crushed between the floors, but we didn't think about it then.

"You didn't think about things like AIDS, either. Bloodborne pathogens—HIV and hepatitis—are serious business, but there were lives to be saved. We just dug in. The broken cement ripped up rubber gloves in moments."

As rescues became retrievals and no more living came to light, however, workers began taking greater precautions.

Danger of contamination on the site was minimal, but persons trained to deal with hazardous materials prefer zero danger whenever possible. People in the white Tyvek suits were the only ones authorized to bag and handle recovered bodies, assuming that whereas the bodies posed a very small risk for handlers, the risk was there. These team members were also prepared to handle dangerous chemicals and other substances, should the rare need arise.

Tough and resilient it may be, but Tyvek doesn't last long. Field-workers got maybe two hours out of a suit before its imperviousness was compromised and it had to be discarded.

Still More Experts

A host of experts other than those in emergency services came to serve. A few of many examples:

Elevator Experts

You don't think about elevators. The signs in hotels and public buildings warn you to use the stairs if fire breaks out; elevators have a disconcerting habit of stopping and opening on the burning floors. As second nature in an emergency, you abandon the elevators. In fact, the freight elevator in the Murrah building was totally disabled; walls had collapsed into the shaft, burying the cage about two floors deep.

The elevators had come to a standstill, the power to the Murrah building cut off. Needless to say, jogging up and down nine floors of stairs gets old in a hurry. Rescue workers and others weren't limited to the stairs for long, though. Oscar Johnson, the manager of the Mid-Western Elevator Company, set to work on what he knows best. Elevators.

At first, Oscar's people at the site helped with the hasty search and initial rescue efforts. Some of them carried several of the children out of the nursery. Then they turned their efforts to the elevators.

Power? Power had been cut off to the building, so they patched a generator into the elevator system. By April 20, a day after the blast, the passenger elevator was working. Now the rescuers, as well as the workers who were stabilizing the junk hanging off the gutted building, could get where they had to go quickly.

Oscar and his workers dug out the freight elevator and got it running a day later. This made it possible for the workers to haul rubble out from the upper stories. From then on until the demolition team came through setting charges, the elevators remained operational. It's an easy thing to take for granted. It wasn't an easy thing to accomplish.[1]

Food Service Experts Who Just Happened to Be in Town

The Oklahoma Restaurant Association was one day into its annual trade show at Myriad Convention Center, its festive premiere event of the year. At 9:02 A.M., about a hundred of the 450 food purveyors exhibiting there were preparing food samples to distribute when the show opened at noon.

Shortly thereafter, the City Fire Department, noting that the fire marshal had come through Myriad the day before and was reporting a lot of food, cooking equipment, and experienced food handlers in place, called Bob Clift. Could his exhibitors possibly prepare lunches for several hundred rescue workers that day?

Within an hour, host Bob Clift and convention chairman Ned Shadid shifted gears. The convention was canceled; it would be irresponsible to attract thousands of people into downtown (they anticipated 12,000 over three days) when emergency work was producing such chaos. In the trade show's place rose a world-class disaster relief center.

The purveyors had spent a bundle for the privilege of exhibiting; yet no one complained about cancellation; no one beefed as they melded into one coordinated operation. Restaurateurs who vied as competitors all year instantly joined forces, working shoulder to shoulder in perfect cooperation.

Normally in the trade show, individual restaurants and suppliers set up dazzling booths to promote their names before buyers in the industry. When the show transformed itself into a relief effort, the promotional aspect absolutely disappeared. Food preparation equipment was pooled; additional equipment, brand new, was brought in and uncrated. The volunteers also were pooled, with no distinction made regarding company or name. Everyone worked where the need was felt.

It was their finest hour.

Those food samples made to woo conferees turned into lunches and were on their way to the site by 11 A.M. The lunch request from the fire department mushroomed into upward of 20,000 meals a day over the next nine days. Up to four assembly lines at a time built meals not just for people in the center but also for people at three rescue-relief shelters nearer the site (one of which was set up to do most of its own cooking). Tons of hot meals, goodie bags, and snacks were shipped out four times a day.

Napoleon claimed that an army travels on its belly. So does a rescue operation. Food is a necessity.

Myriad Convention Center (one part of the floor converted into a warehouse facility) became a distribution center for food donations, accepting shipments and sending them out where needed all over town. Invoices of $10,000 and more came through, but never once did anyone ask, "Who is going to pay for this?"

Says Ned Shadid, "It was very fortunate that this food show was going on. There is no way anyone could have put together an operation like this within an hour."[2]

Fortunate? Perhaps.

But not likely.

God's Experts

The workers clawing their way through the rubble captured the hearts of Oklahoma and the rest of America. Perhaps the response that most impressed the world at large, though, was the unified effort of Oklahoma City's churches. Almost instantly, they were providing food and housing, supplies, practical logistical help, and most of all, spiritual support. Emergency Services—fire, police, and all—were carefully prepared in advance to respond. The many denominations of churches were not thus prepared.

. . . Or were they?

"People from all over Oklahoma City get together for the mayor's annual prayer breakfasts," explains Mark W. Brown, pastor to collegians and young adults at Bethany First Church of the Nazarene. "This year there were 1,200, all concerned about the work of Christ. It's a sort of civic function as well. Certainly they pray, and fervently. There's a guest speaker. They also chat, swap war stories, and exchange suggestions, news, and information. In the lingo of the Christian, they enter into fellowship. In the lingo of the day, they enjoy hanging out together now and then. Call it networking."

Just such a prayer breakfast was held the very morning of the bombing. It dispersed an hour before the tragedy began.

Moments after the blast, Mayor Ron Norick's office called Dr. Robert Allen at Wesley United Methodist Church. "We're going to need chaplains. Can you put together a program?"

He could, but he knew he could not do this alone. He immediately went to the bomb site where he saw Jack Poe, the police department's chaplain. Would he help? Of course, he replied, and he immediately suggested they enlist the aide of Joe Williams, the chaplain for the FBI. They got a handle on specifically what ministry needs would have to be filled. They would find the people to fill those needs and would devise a workable system for getting the assigned chaplains into the inner perimeters of the sealed-off rescue site.

The assignment rapidly expanded into a team effort. Together with several associates, Dr. Allen assisted in building a network of churches to provide ministry to friends and families of all the victims found. He himself took charge of that arm of the effort that provided spiritual support to the relief workers. He would subsequently spend most of his time on site.

Explains Dr. Allen, "First Christian Church seemed a good choice as a clearing house for information and the primary contact point for victims' families. They have the right kind of facilities and enough space. Then we parceled out some of the relief efforts and coordinated with other agencies providing relief. We set up the general plan that would provide chaplains in all the places where we needed them."

Consider: Not all the supplies for the operation could be provided by churches. Other agencies had to handle important parts of it. Overlap was wasteful of time, money, and manpower. Only certain facilities could handle blood donation, for example, but a number of places could provide meals and lodging for rescue workers. Law enforcement was highly specialized and outside the purview of civilians, but those law officers had to be fed and provided for. Where does one agency end and the other begin? A horrific mountain of logistical planning and coordination lay beneath the smooth surface of that operation, and the churches played a primary role.

To appreciate the task, think about to whom you could assign needs as varied as these, were you in charge:

- Lights for the night work and power to operate them
- Chairs for blood centers where lines were a block long
- Triage and first aid supplies
- X-ray equipment sufficient to X-ray each body
- Raincoats, ponchos, umbrellas for all; the weather turned bad
- Dorm space for hundreds of rescue workers
- Comfortable mattresses, cots, or beds (blankets, sheets, and pillowcases) for those hundreds
- Enough porta-potties for everyone, including the media enclave in Satellite City, conveniently placed
- Eye drops, bandages, moleskin, and all the little things to keep the rescuers patched up and in the ring
- Cutting torches and bolt cutters, drills, sledgehammers, crowbars, and more

Every one of those needs was met. And many, many more.

And that's not all. When people need something, they usually need it *now,* not eventually. You have to supply promptly.

But that's just basics. Various agencies made a host of other services available to the workers: haircuts, optical services to replace broken glasses and lost contacts, telephones, a message service, shipping and mailing, physical therapy and sports massage, chiropractic treatments when needed—all provided before the rescue worker's next shift.

And that's *still* not all. There were the hundreds of people made homeless by the blast. For instance, the people living in the four hundred units of the Regency Towers apartment complex, across from the Murrah building, were turned out on the street with nothing save the clothes they were wearing when the building was temporarily declared uninhabitable. Feed the Children, an international organization that just happened to be six miles from the blast site, took care of them with the help of some churches in the area. Hundreds of dazed people—women who had run out of their workplaces without purses, downtown workers whose offices were wrecked and whose vehicles lay fused and mangled—needed somewhere to go. Churches and the Oklahoma Restaurant Association at Myriad Convention Center provided that.

Churches and others met a plethora of needs, but only the Salvation Army was allowed to set up a canteen inside the restricted area. Incidentally, the Salvation Army ended up providing about 3,000 ministers, employees, and volunteers, all told. They counseled 1,600 victims and family members. They figure that long-term needs for people directly affected by the blast will cost about 3.5 million dollars. Feed the Children served 10,000 meals to EMS workers and volunteers. City Church, five blocks away, not all that big a facility, instantly set up food and shelter for relief and rescue workers as well as displaced persons, open twenty-four hours. They served 1,200 to 1,500 meals a day for nearly two weeks.

These figures are typical of the services religious organizations provided. And they did it all on the shortest of notice.

Churches were major coordinators, but not just religious organizations took part in this magnificent, massive effort, of course. For example, the Myriad Convention Center a few blocks away canceled their scheduled conferences and instead housed and fed out-of-state response teams. Myriad became the place where all those displaced downtown workers, most of them stunned and in shock, could come to get off the street. Those people were fed without regard to payment.

Chaplains On-Site

The church network coordinated the services of six hundred chaplains. They developed continuation programs for counsel and support—

loss of this magnitude doesn't heal itself overnight. Even as they were setting up the short-range effort, they were planning the long-range ministry.

Certainly chaplains are expected to comfort the bereaved. But were they considered needed by the rescuers they served? To answer that question let's look at the experience of one chaplain, Pastor Steve Hanchett of Berry Road Baptist Church in Norman, Oklahoma:

"Tuesday night the twenty-fifth, our team was in the street in front of the building. Rescuers had been working diligently to recover one of the Marines. Then the fifty-six members of the team left the building and gathered in the street. One of them came over to me. 'Chaplain, will you pray for us?'

"I assumed that he meant on my own, in private, or with the other chaplains. But as he led me over to the tired, dusty crew, I realized he wanted me to pray with the whole group.

"'Wait a minute, will you?' He got on his radio and asked them to shut down the cranes. He asked the workers up on the rubble pile to pause. He glanced around; he had garnered everyone's attention. 'Now you can pray.'

"Hard hats off and heads bowed, we prayed. In the presence of the FBI, DEA, search and rescue teams, and firemen, we prayed.

"There was no concern about church and state issues, just people in need of God. No doctrinal walls. In the midst of heartache and suffering, there was no shame in praying together in a public place.

"The reality of God.

"I'm humbled by the thought."

And they were not the only workers to feel this way. A call went out to the Critical Incident Stress Debriefing (CISD) team to assist a medical examiner and two rescue workers following the retrieval of a baby's body. The CISD were the pros, right? Trained to handle this sort of thing. Normally, they can. But this time, human wisdom was not sufficient. The medical examiner and rescuers had just taken care of a tiny human being whose flesh had been blasted off the skeleton. No mere professional could ease this pain. They asked specifically for a chaplain.

Yes, God's squad was prepared, just as thoroughly as were the emergency services. The informal network built through the prayer breakfasts shifted seamlessly into a tight, efficient response network to handle all the needs of the rescue operation. The breakfast held that morning covered the network with prayer and galvanized the pastors, preparing them individually for the grueling, relentless job ahead.

They didn't know it was coming. They didn't even know that they were ready.

But they were.

Final Analysis

The final chapter is far from being written. The psychological and economic effects of the bombing will be with us for years to come. But already, emergency response systems around the world are looking at the lessons Oklahoma City offers them. They're calling it the Oklahoma Standard. What worked? What didn't?

In the aftermath of the bombing, when Monday-morning quarterbacks manage to find the little mistakes that escaped those playing in the heat of the game, nearly everyone agreed: Almost everything worked. The operation had flowed nearly flawlessly despite the enormous emotional toll, not to mention the abundant opportunity for personality problems and control issues to get in the way of the job.

Chief Marrs attributes the success to a top-notch department and thorough preparation, perhaps not realizing that he speaks for God's team as well as his own.

CHAPTER FOUR

The Miracle of the Supernatural

MINUTES AFTER IT HAPPENED, CINDY Katterson relayed the grim news of the Murrah bombing to her sister Judy in North Carolina. If the phone cord had given her an electrical shock, she couldn't have been more surprised by her sister's response: "Can you imagine the angels that were there?"

Cindy was surprised by this comment. "As a Christian, I believe in the intervention of these emissaries of God in the history of humankind, but that was head knowledge. The thought of their presence or activity in downtown Oklahoma City that morning had never crossed my mind. And then I heard Barbara Rickner's story."

Barbara Rickner was busy fixing hams and desserts to serve at the funeral of a relative in the church family. When the TV announced the bombing, she was stunned. But she had an obligation, so she hurriedly dressed, loaded the meal into her Oldsmobile, and took off.

At 10:30 she was driving up over I-40 on the Harrah-Newalla overpass. The bombing, of course, was preying on her mind. "I looked over westward toward Oklahoma City, twenty miles away," Barbara remembers. "The city was much too distant to see anything, but I was looking anyway.

"Instantly I slowed the car to a crawl and rolled the window down. A huge cloud rested over the city skyline. It was brilliant white interspersed with shades of soft white and gray. The hair stood up on the back of my neck. That cloud was filled with hundreds of angels' wings!

"Once I was off the overpass, I didn't have the elevation to see well anymore, and trees obstructed my view. I could still see the top of the cloud, though. All the angels were facing west. Long wings of incredible dimension trailed gracefully behind their backs.

"I heard myself whisper, 'Oh, Lord, there must be a multitude of angels!'"

Angels standing silent vigil over the ruins of the Murrah building.

Comfort by Supernatural Agents

God, claim the theologians, speaks to different people in different ways according to their culture, needs, and interests. At the birth of Jesus Christ, He hit the shepherds over the head with brilliant light (all the brighter for happening at night) and a host of angels. To the Chaldean magi He sent a single star. Both messages were appropriately received and acted upon. The way God will speak to you is not the way He will speak to me.

Christian theologians also point out that any working of God's Holy Spirit counts as a supernatural event. There agreement ends. To what extent the Spirit operates, and whether such things as angels even enter today's world, are all matters of much debate.

Theology aside, witnesses report a number of supernatural events occurring at the moment of the bombing or soon thereafter. Without exception, these manifestations provided comfort rather than fear, peace rather than concern. Certainly many of the stories are apocryphal—"a friend of a friend had this cousin who. . . ."

Apocryphal stories, unsubstantiated when one tries to track them down, sometimes take on a life of their own, growing into what are called "urban myths." No doubt a goodly number of such unsubstantiated myths are bound to arise from the rubble of the Murrah building. Most people tend to discount these tales, and with good reason. Such things ought to be verifiable.

People also discount the testimony of wackos—that is, persons perceived by their expressed thoughts and behavior to be slightly daft folk whose driveways don't quite reach the street. Again, there is justification for doubting the testimony.

But when ordinary people such as the woman above spontaneously offer firsthand observations, there is no sound reason not to believe them.

And she is not alone.

Patrice Hutchison offers this account of what happened on April 19:

"I felt the blast in a protected building two blocks away. I was standing by windows in a solid, thirty-story structure, facing away from the direction of the explosion. I happened to be looking out across a park, admiring the many shades of green.

"Solid or not, our building swayed. I could see the force move through the trees and hit the buildings beyond; a reflection of a monument in the park seemed to move across the mirrored facade of one of those buildings and then return to its usual place.

"We bolted out of the building and across the street to that park. A few minutes later we were told it was all right to return to the building. Then they said another bomb had been located. We were told to leave the area. 'Don't try going north,' they said. 'Traffic is all backed up.'

"It felt strange to be going home in the middle of the day, as if I were playing hooky. I drove south, then west several miles before heading north. Where was all the traffic? It seemed as if the world had stopped.

"On an overpass just west of downtown, I looked back for the first time toward where it had happened, and to where I had just been. It seemed as if a great deal of time had passed or maybe no time at all. It was hard to tell.

"Tiny white somethings were hovering, sort of suspended, above the area of the Alfred P. Murrah building. Although I cannot say why or how I knew this, nor do I understand, I accepted without a doubt that these were supernatural beings. I assumed they were the spirits of the souls, as I understand it, of some of the ones whose bodies were destroyed by the blast.

"The sight didn't upset me in any way. In fact, I recall a peace. They seemed natural. Even expected.

"I had to turn my attention to the road for a moment. I looked again to confirm what I had seen. They were still there and I smiled. I remember that, as I drove on, I only questioned why they weren't zooming away toward another place. This is what I thought would happen if they were souls released from their earthly bodies.

"But there they were, just being, watching. Could they be angels?"

Ms. Hutchison is thoroughly reliable. There is no reason to impugn her testimony.

Neither is there any reason to discount the story which the mother of a six-year-old tells. When the mother picked up her daughter at the baby-sitter's on April 19, the child told her, "I saw an angel!"

The little girl had heard about the bombing soon after it happened and had been noticeably upset.

Says the mother, "She said that as she was swinging on the swing set, an angel in the sky told her they were coming for the babies. That made her feel so much better, and that makes me feel so much better too."

A plethora of unverifiable stories abound. For example, it is purported that a survivor of the blast claims something or someone shoved her chair back a split second before her desk and everything else plunged down into the pit. The agent is commonly identified as an angel.

Are none true? Are all? The skeptic sneers at his or her peril. If it is indeed the hand of God, it's not wise to snicker.

Remember too that each incident stands on its own. If some are true, that does not mean they all are. If one is discounted, that does not mean they can all be discounted.

The Ministry of Angels

From reports like these in Oklahoma City and from God's Word, we can develop a picture of what we think angels might be.

Angels are created beings, apparently of great intelligence. No person's encounter with an angel, either in Scripture or in life, suggests that they are anything less than commanding in their intellectual grasp and understanding.

Angels are spirit beings, which is to say that in their normal form they have no form. In technical terms, they are non-corporeal. No body. This poses a problem for us corporeal beings who can normally only see the material. On certain occasions, and we have no way of knowing why angels choose one occasion over another, angels solve our problem for us by taking a visible form.

Forget the chubby little baby you see on Christmas cards. Angels, even cherubim, are awesome. Angels sometimes appear as angels—terrifying seraphim such as Ezekiel describes in his chapter one. They may appear as human beings. Most Hebrew scholars count as angels the men who visited Abraham by the oaks of Mamre in Genesis 18. Gideon didn't seem to recognize the angel who spoke to him in Judges 6:11. Judges 13 records what is probably a typical encounter with angels. The conclusion seems to be that if angels wish, they can appear in quite ordinary human likeness.

Angels, most people agree, have no barriers between themselves and God. They do His will completely. When they say, "God says," you'd better believe God says. When they appear, they are representing God. And that's just what they seemed to be doing in Oklahoma City on April 19.

Other Supernatural Occurrences

In addition to reports of angels, several verifiable stories have surfaced about symbols of God's presence, visions, and other means of comfort. Some firemen who entered the building the first night noticed that the only lights in one area formed a perfect cross. "Well, it looks like the Man has this area covered," one said to the other.

Valerie Koelsch's aunt tells this story:

Valerie's mother, Rosemary, was out of town on April 19. The moment she heard about the bombing, she made haste to get home. Valerie worked at the Federal Employees Credit Union in that building, and Rosemary was frantic.

Then thunderstorms delayed her flight from Dallas to Oklahoma City and her anxiety was multiplied by frustration.

Stuck with nowhere to go, Rosemary let her mind drift to thoughts of home, and of Valerie's golden hair. Valerie's face took visible form in front of Rosemary; her blonde hair glowed. Rosemary basked in a radiance no one else seemed to notice.

"Mom, I'm okay." It was Valerie's voice, Valerie's face.

Again, "Mom, I'm okay."

Days later, the crushed body of Valerie Koelsch was retrieved from the stack of collapsed floors.

But that was only her body. Her mom and dad knew she was okay.[1]

Priscilla Salyers received her comfort in quite a different context. She was at her desk in the U.S. Customs Service complex, the desk closest to the hall, when her coworker Paul Ice said something indistinct.

She turned. "What did you say?"

All of a sudden the world exploded. They made a moment of eye contact—powerful eye contact, Priscilla recalls. Then flashing lights, a tunnel effect, the wind. She thought the sensation of falling which she felt was her head dropping forward onto her desk. She was experiencing some sort of seizure, obviously.

She had never lost consciousness, exactly, but now full awareness was returning. She was totally pinned. There was no digging out, no squirming. She could move only her left arm and hand.

But her free hand was clasping someone else's warm hand. She was not alone. That simple fact—she was not alone—comforted her beyond describing. *She was not alone.*

Voices in the distance said that a day care was near. Near? The day-care center was down on the second floor, and she was up on the fifth. Not until much later would she learn that the whole Customs office had been sheered off and dumped into the pit. She had fallen with the rest of it, from the fifth floor to the edge of the pile at about first-floor level. Somehow she miraculously survived that plunge.

Another voice said he was getting someone out. She waved her arm, the only thing that could move.

Nearer to her, someone else called out, "We have a live one!"

A rescuer grasped her flapping hand and asked her name. She was safe. Then: "Priscilla, we have to leave. Sorry. We have to go get more tools." No one at that time mentioned to her the bomb scare that nearly cleared the building.

Furious about being summarily left like that, she determined to survive this thing, whatever it was. After an eternity or two, her rescuers returned. She was extricated at 1:15 P.M., a little over four hours after that near-fatal plunge.

Three days later, she learned that the hand she held at first, the warm touch that told her she was not alone and gave her such powerful comfort, was that of a corpse.

Her shock. Her grief for that person—and the others who died that day—seemed overpowering.

Robert Wise and his wife, Margueritte, who is also a minister, visited Priscilla in the hospital.

As Robert was praying for her, he felt the Holy Spirit prompting him to help her see that hand as the hand of Jesus. Not so far-fetched. In a very real respect, the vision was the greater part of truth. The source of comfort was God; the means, or tool, was the hand.

God also had words of comfort for many others in Oklahoma City the Sunday after the bombing.

The Comfort of a Word

You'd have thought it was Easter, the way Oklahoma's churches were packed that Sunday. People came loaded with grief and mourning, and hoping for respite.

Following a service of communion, praise, and prayer at Church of the Redeemer, one of the members asked to speak a word from God to the body of believers.

Now a bit of explanation is due here. Certain believers in the Christian church are called charismatics, from the Greek word *charisma* meaning *gift*. The word refers to special gifts which the charismatics claim are bestowed by the Holy Spirit over and above the basic and essential gift of salvation. One of those gifts is termed *prophecy* and refers not to foretelling the future so much as to delivering God's present word to His people, usually in a church setting. The member who asked to speak that morning was known in his congregation as a person whom God used for that purpose.

His word:

> I have felt your sorrow and I have seen your tears, and I have wept over your city. But I want you to know those who knew Me are with Me, and the children are in My care, and they are safe with Me. And I want you to know that as you see all of the numbers of rescuers and helpers there, that I have even many more of My angels that are there, and they are also ministering and caring for you. Know that I love you and I know the sorrow you are feeling, but I want you to know that I will be glorified in this. That I will have victory in this; and you will see that I will take all that is bad and turn it to your benefit and to My glory.

A week later, the leader of a charismatic congregation on the other side of the city was visiting that speaker's home, noticed the message typed out, and picked it up to read it. He gasped. "This is *exactly* the same message that we received in our congregation Sunday morning, word for word!"

God's comfort.

The Hebrew psalmists tried their best, but they only partially convey the comfort which God provides. Above all else, our God is a God of comfort. Many and diverse were the means of comfort He provided in Oklahoma City.

But there is a flip side.

The Other Side of Comfort

A number of theologians who have explored the nature of God to the extent that it can be known to human understanding claim that He hurts as powerfully as He loves. Some people form weak attachments with other persons. They don't love powerfully, but then they don't seem to hurt powerfully when, inevitably, loss occurs. People who care deeply hurt deeply.

Students of God carry this observation, along with God's own words that He made men and women in His likeness, to the logical conclusion: God cares more than any human being can perceive; therefore He hurts more than any human being can perceive.

Almost no one, when quizzed right after the bombing, blamed the tragedy on God. Nearly everyone hoped and prayed that good would come of it, beauty from the ashes. Not many stopped then to consider how much God might be hurting, empathetically sharing the pain of the bereaved.

We're considering that now.

This poem, written by Bev Sumner, was distributed at First Christian Church, where families were waiting for some word about the persons still missing.

Nothing gave any warning that morning!
There was no time, or place, to hide. . . .
A bomb brought the walls and floors
crashing down
And in heaven all the angels cried!

Tears and sweat streaked the bloody faces,
As many hands reached to help those inside . . .
Bringing out injured people from everywhere
And silently, the angels cried!

A tiny toddler drew much attention there
While lying in a fireman's arms it died. . . .
Stunned adults, broken and bleeding stood back,
These too explain why the angels cried!

Emergency crews swarmed over the scene
to a building hundreds daily occupied. . . .
They found a task without beginning, or end,
And still, God's angels cried!

Another child was carried out by a medic,
and from his grasp she had to be pried . . .
As he held on tightly to her security,
Yes, even this little angel cried!

While the world watched in shocked disbelief
In Oklahomans they all took pride. . . .
And those days of rain, was not rain, you see
It was really the tears all the angels cried![2]

The Miracle of Ordinary People Doing the Extraordinary

LEIGH ANN MORRILL IS A NURSE, BUT she wasn't working on April 19. She was home on vacation, just goofing around, when the boom rocked her house.

"I ducked," she remembers. "In my own home (I live seven or eight miles west of the site), I ducked, it was so startling. I ran out front and all my neighbors were out front too, looking at each other. 'What was that?' So I went back in and turned on the TV immediately.

"They were asking for medical people, so I called the hospital and they told me they were on disaster alert. I grabbed my pager and hopped in the car.

"I didn't have a clue how I was going to get there; I just began driving. I distinctly remember praying, 'Well, Lord, here I am. Use me as You need me.' I assumed I'd get caught in a traffic jam pretty soon. I kind of figured I'd just drive until I couldn't get any closer. I got closer and closer. I was finally stopped by a police line—right at a great parking spot.

"I hadn't even seen the site yet, but I was dazed. Even from here, some blocks away, windows were blown out of buildings. Debris lay all over. And glass on the ground. So much glass.

"About then I happened onto a group of people hurrying toward the site and joined them. There were maybe ten of us, obviously medical person-nel. The others were carrying boxes of dressings, bandages, airways, tape, respiratory equipment, and I wondered why I didn't bring anything. I should have been carrying supplies in too. One of the nurses gave me a couple of pairs of rubber gloves.

"Some of the people in this group were from nearby hospitals, but a couple were from Normal Regional. That's thirty or forty miles away! They said when they heard, they just piled into a van and came on up to make themselves available.

"It was the most incredible thing, walking in with this group. None of the talk was idle chatter. We each told our specialties; this woman was an emergency room nurse, that doctor was a pediatrician. So by the time we got there, we all knew what expertise was available—who did what.

"We arrived at a parking lot where the police directed us and set up a triage center. It was maybe 11 A.M. now. A firefighter there told us about what to expect, based on what they'd dealt with so far. Some pretty horrible things.

"One of the nurses said, 'I have children of my own. I don't know how I'm going to handle this.'

"Immediately, a nurse beside me said, 'We need to pray.' What a wonderful thing! Right there in the parking lot, we prayed for the rescuers, the victims, and us."

A little explanation here. Triage is sorting, so to speak. Say you're injured in a disaster. You arrive at a triage center first where the nurses and doctors get your name and take a quick look at you. If you have an obvious, life-threatening injury, you go right to the head of the line for fast attention. If your injuries are not life-threatening, you're treated after the worst-hurt people. That way you don't have someone dying of, say, internal injuries because they had to wait while someone with hangnails was being attended.

"We weren't there at 9:30 to receive the first wave. That's what the firefighter told us about. We were anticipating getting the second wave, as they dug to a point where they thought victims would be found. Nothing. We stood around.

"About 1:30, twenty-five or thirty of us walked in to the south side of the Murrah building and set up again. We thought maybe we hadn't been getting any patients because we were too far away. But we didn't get any more. There weren't any more.

"I can't begin to describe the incredible community outpouring, and it was almost instantaneous. You had double-file bucket brigades, office people working bare-handed with their shirtsleeves rolled up. Everybody, in uniform and not, were removing debris, digging for people who might be alive.

"We were waiting around, hoping for anyone alive, and not really knowing what was happening in there. It was so frustrating. Then a fire department chaplain came out and told us what was going on, keeping us informed. Isn't that great? That chaplain was ministering to us. We were there to help, and he was helping us, giving us exactly what we needed just then.

"I can't describe what a wonderful feeling it was to watch people coming from everywhere, making themselves available, wanting to help. The bombing was a horrible thing that hurt and impacted so many lives. I'm not minimizing that. But I also just want to climb the tallest building in Oklahoma City and shout, 'Yesss!'"

Making Oneself Available

"Swing your bat," some say, "and let God run the bases you can't reach." Over and over and over again, the same theme played out. Ordinary people offered themselves without reservation for whatever needed doing and did what they could do. Their seemingly random efforts, little bits of heart music here and there, became a beautifully orchestrated symphony, many instruments singing in harmony. Examples:

The Girl Who Captured the Moment with a Sign

The rescue effort was less than a day old so far. Cyndy McGarr sat quietly among many people of all stripes and persuasions at the volunteer post, awaiting some task. This was the beginning of a nightmare no one could define. No one knew how long it would last. Some whispered, "Weeks, maybe."

Sitting here, she felt a strong spiritual power surging through the body of workers, something transcending human effort. She couldn't define it, but she couldn't find anyone else with words to define it either. No one in the media had mentioned it. Only the people here on-site seemed to know it existed.

It certainly wasn't the surroundings. Ten-foot chain-link fence around the ragged ruin, stark white floodlights, the generators whirring like helicopters. Concentration camp maybe. War zone certainly. But not a spiritual place. And yet . . .

How to convey some measure of this spirit?

Not too certain herself about what to do, she unrolled some butcher paper and created a sign. It read:

We're here and we're committed.
We are steadfast and strong in our combined strengths.
We're Oklahomans,
And we're not leaving until this job is done.
God be with our nation.

She would hang it up on that sterile, iron-cold chain-link fence. Then she made a second:

Pray for those still trapped.
Pray for those who've lost family.
Pray for those helping.
Pray for our enemies.

Halfway through, she stopped. She was outside the compound that a nation was watching. Security had tightened considerably in the last few hours. She was putting her prayer up in a world where prayer is omitted and even berated more times than not. She'd never been more proud to be a Christian, but she felt more than a little shaky. This could be Violating-the-Constitution stuff. She could just imagine someone wrenching her Magic Marker out of her hand and making an example of her.

And then she happened to glance back over her shoulder.

The workers who had just come off their twelve-hour shift were standing grouped at the fence, watching her. Their backs to the shattered building, their faces sweaty, they were waiting for Cyndy to finish her prayer sign.

Whatever she might be expecting, this wasn't it! She froze. She couldn't get her pen to touch the paper.

Then a voice as if it were Jesus whispered, "Go ahead. I told you what to say. Say it. It's simple. It needs to be said. It's resting on their hearts and minds too."

She finished her sign:

Pray not only for Oklahoma and
Oklahomans,
But also for our nation and our world.
Pray all these things earnestly in Jesus' name.
God be with us all.

The firefighters, with their bunker hats in their hands, nodded to her and wiped their faces as they walked away.

The next day she polished her makeshift prayer a little, trying to help it reach the non-Christian eye and heart. *What I'd really like to do,* she thought, *is put it on some T-shirts to give the workers.* A little hitch: She didn't have a job or a cent.

Kinko's downtown. They did T-shirts. She took her prayer there, having no clear idea yet that her God was moving through this entire enterprise. To her reasoning mind, this was dumb. She stepped out beyond reason.

Kinko's did the shirts up and donated the first dozen. Contributions provided two hundred more. Her project was on its way.

Long after rain had melted away the first sign, the second, the volunteer's prayer, remained, draped among the flowers on the fence.

Volunteers and More Volunteers

Bill Hamiter, an associate minister at Bethany First Church of the Nazarene as well as a Red Cross volunteer, called Cindy Overholt, the secretary to the senior pastor. "We need nine volunteers to work the late shift, 10 P.M. to 6 A.M."

She called two students, Scott Martin and Kevin Hackler, asking them and seven others of their choice to work the night shift.

Twenty-seven people showed up at the bus.

The eighteen extras simply made themselves available and ended up filling important jobs. Nine served at the Red Cross post. Some helped out at Feed the Children and others at City Church, where they were keeping kitchens open.

This story in various forms repeated itself over and over. People volunteered unstintingly for the most menial tasks, whether day or graveyard shift. "God is love," Scripture proclaims. Love poured out in the form of prayer and service. It became one of the most stirring testimonies to the spirit of God. Within days, there were more volunteers than work.

Brad Yarbrough, pastor at Grace Community Church, reports: "Two van loads of students from a local Christian college pulled up in front of First Christian Church at about 3:00 A.M. What could they do to help? Clean the church? What could they do? We asked them where they'd been. They'd been singing hymns for the rescue workers all evening."

The Yellow Roses

Joni Eareckson Tada, a quadriplegic whose greeting cards and books are an inspiration to many, writes about witnessing a tiny vignette of human nature:

"After [a visit to First Christian Church], some officials took us to the bomb site. I could hardly stand to look up into the ragged guts of the building. I glanced away and noticed a man and woman approaching with a glass vase of beautiful roses. I recognized them from the family center— they were relatives of a woman named Oleta whose body was trapped somewhere on the second floor. Oleta's husband, Hank, had wanted to bring the yellow roses to the bomb site, but instead he sent his relatives to carry the vase. Hank just couldn't bring himself to deliver the roses personally.

"They handed the vase of thick, fresh roses to a chaplain who was standing near me and asked, 'Could someone please take these flowers and place them on the second floor?'

"The chaplain and the roses disappeared and within minutes, I spotted through the chain-link fence the crystal vase being gingerly carried toward the building between the chaplain and a tall fireman. They disappeared behind a pile of concrete and an earthmover.

"Maybe it's because I'm an artist. Maybe it's because I have eyes of faith. Whatever the reason, I have never seen yellow look so . . . *yellow*! Amidst all the orange earthmovers, red flags, brown dirt, gray concrete, and blue coats of FBI workers sifting through the rubble, that bouquet of yellow roses shone with beautiful iridescence. A tiny vase of flowers that symbolized 'hope' and 'love' and 'family unity.' The roses stuck out like a beautiful thumb against the ugly sore spot of bomb-blasted rubble. That sharp, crystalline image of yellow roses will remain in my memory for years to come—an unfading picture that all the world's hate, malice, and wickedness can never, *ever* discolor."

Flowers and Help for the Children

On another occasion, a grief-stricken man approached Dr. Allen. His wife and son had just been buried the day before. Joe Williams, the FBI Chaplain, had officiated the service. "Is it all right to bring flowers?"

"Of course! Did you bring them?"

"Uh . . . no," said the haggard man. "I'll have to get some."

At that moment, City Councilman Mark Schwartz brought in a beautiful arrangement sent from Denver, Colorado. A cascade of flowers cradled a teddy bear. The message: "For the children of Oklahoma City."

The man was escorted to the gate, and officials carried the flowers in and placed them at the bomb sight.

Dr. Allen still beams as he relates that tale. "To think that the appropriate arrangement arrived at just that moment when it was most needed!"

Flowers for the children in the path of the bomb. And help for those who were indirect victims. The day after the bombing, a pastor was watching the continuous coverage when a reporter on camera spoke to children who might be watching. "Here's the number to call if your parents have not returned yet."

"Until that moment," the pastor recalls, "I didn't realize fully the lives that were impacted—the human toll." And this pastor had been in the midst of it from the beginning. "But also it brought home to me the many ways we all provided comfort. Here might be children alone. They had someone to turn to."

Neighbors spontaneously took over children's care when parents failed to show, or when one parent was down at the scene awaiting word on another.

Entertainment for the Children at First Christian

Children of trapped victims get as bored and restless as any others. The kids milling around in the First Christian Church's Family Assistance Center, awaiting word that would almost certainly be tragic, needed diversion and cheer more than most.

Enter Charlie, a spider monkey, and Shelly, a mixed-breed dog. End of boredom.

The snub-nosed Charlie mugs, hugs, snuggles, and shakes hands as only a spider monkey can. Shelly, the dog, happens to be deaf; noisy crowds don't bother her.

Shelly and Charlie's owner, Sharlotte Campbell, looks on her animals as great stress relievers. Kids, even older kids, are totally dependent upon their parents. When a parent dies, a child's whole world craters. Sharlotte more than most realizes the devastation, for she counsels children. "Kids have to get back to the here and the now. These animals can bring back their feelings."

Case in point, a young child who had lost a parent in the blast: The child had neither spoken nor eaten for days. Sharlotte showed up by invitation at the child's home, Charlie the spider monkey on her shoulder. By degrees, the ice thawed, the wall cracked. Before long, the child was talking to the monkey, giggling, and playing.[1]

You do what you can do, even if you're a nine-month-old spider monkey. God grants the increase.

Humor in the Midst of Sorrow

Argus Hamilton writes a humor column for the *Daily Oklahoman.* So do you cancel humor in this time of tears? Argus understands the power of gentle humor to ease loss. Calling laughter a vaccine, he redoubled efforts to bring a little light to Oklahoma's darkest hour. The first paragraph of his column would routinely offer an uplifting sentiment; the remainder would poke pins into pompous balloons and roast nonsensical decisions. Presidents and politicians, celebrities and sports figures got skewered, and usually deserved it. . . . but *never* anyone associated with the rescue effort.

Encouragement from the Very Youngest

In Edmond, second-graders reasoned that hospitalized young victims might not be able to hold a book or even to see. So they made a tape of stories, songs, and poems for them. They read a book and created their own stories and poems. They made worry dolls and get-well cards, then sent the gifts to the hospitals.

Symbols of Encouragement

Marcia Spivey was one of the volunteers at the Myriad Convention Center, where rescuers were being housed and fed. Normally, she worked the food line. There she met Caroline Morton. Instant soul mates, the women decided these rescuers needed the touch of true southern hospitality. Each night, they placed something on the pillows of the men and women who worked at the site—a mint, gum, candy, letters from schoolkids, teddy bears.

Rescue personnel needed only mention some need, Marcia or one of the other volunteers would get on the cellular phone and start calling around. The volunteers, the whole city, the whole state, the whole nation were making themselves available.

Says Marcia, "I'm a structured individual. When I found they had a need, I tried to fulfill it."

On one day, weary returning rescuers found a beautiful red flower on their pillow, courtesy of Project Aloha in Hawaii.

Rescuers called the Myriad, "The Five Star Resort for Rescuers."

For further example, laundry services downtown provided free cleaning to several FEMA teams. Nuway Laundry, an allied member of the Oklahoma Restaurant Association, scrambled to turn the out-of-town rescuers' laundry around in twelve hours in time for the the next shift. Sorting through a pile, one of the laundry workers found several hundred dollars in a pocket. This was a couple weeks' take-home pay for that lady.

She didn't have the slightest idea whose pants these were, but she knew they were in a twelve hour batch. Imagine the rescuer's surprise when the laundry found the owner and gave his money back to him.

And then there was the genuine, unspendable Oklahoma dollar, which is one of Oklahoma City police chaplain Jack Poe's favorite stories.

"I was talking to one of the rescuers who had come in from New York City. He was a veteran of the World Trade Center rescue operation.

"He said, 'Look here. I have an unspendable Oklahoma dollar,' and he pulled out this dollar bill. 'I came here with expense money. I can't spend it. Nobody will take it. You fed me, clothed me, and sheltered me for free. You even cut my hair for free. One time working the Trade Center, I had to pay ten dollars for a hamburger. I cannot believe the love you have here.

"'Anyway, this is an Oklahoma dollar.'

"The governor, Frank Keating, got wind of it. He wrote 'Authentic Unspendable Oklahoma Dollar' across the bill and signed it."

T-Shirts for Nameless Saints

One day Marcia Spivey saw a T-shirt with a firefighter, policeman, medical worker, and dog. None had a face. The inscription on back: "We give our thanks. The hundreds of people who gave it their all, without personal or individual acknowledgement." She saw that it was by Artistic Designs in the City. Marcia and Caroline Morton set out to raise the money for a nameless saint T-shirt for each person who helped in the rescue effort.

This was a bigger project than they realized. They ended up founding the Disaster Hospitality Care Team to handle donations and make and distribute the shirts. They were subsequently invited by FEMA (Federal Emergency Management Agency) to the "National Donation Conference" in Boston. To deliver personal thanks, they traveled to each of the eleven cities who had sent workers at their own expense.

Ribbons of Encouragement

Ribbons turned up all over the city. Everyone had one and every ribbon was created by a volunteer. They sat on curbs making ribbons to hand out on the spot. They sat by their television sets in the evenings making them to distribute later. Thousands of ribbons.

At first, a ribbon was intended to say, "I have a loved one involved in this effort," and the color indicated the nature of that involvement. In no time at all, people emotionally involved—but not directly connected to the incident—were wearing them too. The meaning rapidly expanded to, "I am thinking about you. I am praying for you."

The colors, symbolically:

Purple ribbons indicated the children. In classic symbolism, purple denotes royalty, children of a King. Parents of missing children might wear them. But many—so many others ached for the children—that soon numbers of people sported them.

Green meant prayer. Green is the color of hope and rebirth. Pastors, radio announcers, and others urged all those who believed in God to display a green ribbon, telling the world they were in prayer.

White indicated concern for the innocents slaughtered. White symbolizes purity. Many wore white ribbons to give expression to the innocence of those lost. Certainly the children were innocent. But no adult in the building deserved what happened either.

Blue is Oklahoma's color; Oklahoma's flag features symbols of peace on a blue background. Blue symbolizes virtue. Those who wore blue were expressing pride in their state and in the way Oklahomans responded. It was not an egotistic pride. It was humble pride.

Red came to reflect the emergency services—fire and rescue, blood and flame. Red symbolizes ardor and extreme emotion. Many, many supporters of the public services used red ribbons to voice their appreciation.

Red, white, and blue combined ribbons indicated everything the individual colors symbolize plus a national pride. Said one woman who wore the combined ribbon: "Something like this doesn't detract from our nation a bit. It shows what we're made of, and I could not be more proud!"

The Photographer Who Touched the World

Probably the best-known "gifted amateur" to serve the purposes of God in the effort is Chuck Porter. He did so simply by making himself available.

When the bomb exploded, business pretty well came to a halt. Chuck Porter was working in the loan department of a bank nearby. Because he's an amateur photographer, he grabbed his camera and ran the two and one-half blocks to see what had happened.

He arrived thirteen minutes after the explosion. Police had already established a perimeter on the north side, but there was still plenty of opportunity to shoot the action. Between 9:15 and 10, Chuck clicked them off, not really certain what he was getting, or even that his efforts were sufficiently focused.

When his film ran out, he took it to the one-hour photo lab at Wal-Mart. The employees realized they were pictures of the explosion aftermath. "Can we see them?"

Chuck had no idea what was on his film until he saw the employees' eyes fill with tears. He was beginning to grasp the idea that these images were powerful. He called a photographer friend. "What do I do?"

"Take them to the Associated Press Bureau in Oklahoma City—*now!*"

He had to look the number up in the phone book and get a map to find the location. It was about 11:00 A.M.

He got home at 1:30 P.M. A few minutes later, a call came from the *London Times,* that respected and dignified old maiden aunt of the world's newspapers. Confused, he asked, "Why are you calling me?"

"Don't you know? Tomorrow, your photograph is going to be on the front page of just about every newspaper on earth."

Of his two photos taken in sequence, the first is of a police officer handing a fragile child over to a fireman. In the second, now known around the world, the fireman is cradling tiny Baylee Almon in his arms.

After that photo was published, Chuck received a startling number of hate calls and letters. He hadn't been expecting anything like that. They arrived from all over the country. They accused him of using a terrible situation to feather his own nest. They accused him of exploitation of the most disgusting, degrading kind. (If anyone does *not* deserve that sort of smear, it's Chuck. He is one of the wisest, most humble people.) It put him on a downer and generated all sorts of guilt; what if they were right and he had been wrong? What if, as some of these callers suggested, he had really offended God? He loved God. The last thing in the world he'd want to do was. . . .

And then came a letter from Chester, Vermont. Handwritten, it was addressed to:

Charles Porter
Bank Nearest the Bomb Site
Oklahoma City, Oklahoma

That was all.

Right there, one of God's miracles kicked in: Chuck received it only a couple of days after it was sent. Anyone in the postal service will tell you that's impossible.

At the moment when he needed it most, Chuck received a message that put his feelings into words exactly and really made him think:

> *I am writing you this letter because I have a message for you. . . . God knows you can do it. You have been tested many times and have come through for good ways. . . . We know that fear knocks out God and this is what will be used on you. When you feel this coming on, ask for God's help. He will send help from above.*

Chuck often says how immensely grateful he is to the sender of that letter. The timing, the letter itself—God's grace through the whole matter—buoyed his spirits and put him on the track again.

The Man Who Didn't Run from the Second Bomb Scare

Mike Walker, a firefighter intermediate paramedic, talked to us about those first hectic hours as shocked and bleeding survivors poured out into the street.

"We had in excess of fifty patients in triage, and a guy said to me, 'This lady needs an IV.' He was right; she was looking shocky and her vitals were slipping. She was lying on the ground outside the building.

"I didn't know if he was qualified to handle intravenous, and things were slowing down enough, so I said, 'Let me start it.'

"Suddenly, here's all these people running toward us, screaming and shouting. A thundering herd. It was because of that second bomb scare; they were running for their lives. We couldn't move this lady just yet, and I was worried we'd be trampled. Marcus Evans, a recruit, threw a bunker coat over me as protection.

"I looked at the people who were still standing around and said, 'If you guys aren't Christians, you'd better run.'"

Now, weeks later, we asked him why *he* didn't run.

"I just couldn't leave her," he said.

Mike has more to say, important things. "The thing people need to realize is, if none of the firefighters or police officers or rescue workers showed up at all, the people who needed help would have gotten it. There were people shaving that morning, who if they cut themselves would be squeamish. Two hours later, those same people were battle-hardened medics. Not once did I see anyone panic. It was beyond emotion. All kinds of so-called ordinary folks did things they didn't think they could do. And they couldn't! It was God.

"Those people, the ones who didn't survive, went to work that day thinking it would be business as usual. When we found the bodies, most of them were in huddles. Groups. And I can only imagine that they were sitting around doing whatever you do. It is so important for people to realize that even if they're sitting reading this book, that they could die. Any moment.

"God loves us, He's proven that. The question is not, 'How could a loving God do this?' but, 'How could such a loving God love such evil people?'"

All of these stories show ordinary people doing the extraordinary, just as Mike Walker says.

Do these seemingly unrelated incidents constitute miracles? Some think so. Maybe little miracles, but in the scheme of things there is no size comparison when it comes to miracles. These and a thousand other incidents are certainly strong evidence of God's movement and providence. From the tremendous response and desire to be available, these people show that there is no doubt He was there from the start, producing heroes.

Jon Hansen, assistant chief of the Oklahoma City Fire Department, says, "The heroes are those who are working long hours on a volunteer basis.

We are paid for our efforts, but the volunteers give from their hearts countless hours of service."[2]

We do what we can do.

CHAPTER SIX

The Miracle of Comfort to Servants on the Edge

PHYLLIS POE AND HER HUSBAND, JACK, the police department chaplain, were both down at the site not long after the bomb went off. They had a contact point set up in a corner of the telephone company building, where chaplains could go one-on-one with rescue workers on site.

An officer came in, garbed in fire department gear, wearing a bandanna, and carrying a box sort of thing. They had seen him at the site earlier, and Jack had talked to him many times.

"Do you know what that box is?" Jack asked Phyllis.

"No," she answered.

"An infrared camera. The man is a police department chopper pilot who up 'til now has used infrared equipment to fly over an area and find persons at night. The human body puts off heat, and his apparatus can pick that up. They are trying to use the apparatus to find bodies and possibly living victims in the rubble. This is the first time anyone has attempted this particular technique. In fact, they're going to write a paper on it.

"Yesterday this officer told me he was down in the basement, peering into the rubble with his infrared device. He came upon the face of a little boy about three with his eyes open and his hands sort of up. They determined the child was dead. But those eyes. This man had a three-year-old of his own and it really got to him. Absolutely tore him up."

The man saw the Poes and grabbed Phyllis by the hand. He said, "You've got to pray with me."

"Okay. Sure. Let's go over there." Phyllis indicated a sofa in the corner. They settled there close together.

The man seemed distraught. "I have to go back down there. I need your prayers," he said.

"A simple bowing of the head didn't seem enough just now," Phyllis said. "I put my arms around him and almost immediately felt bigger arms encompassing us both. It was Jack.

"We prayed with the man. After our prayer, he went back down where he was needed. He's that seasoned a professional. That man with his device located sixty-four bodies in the debris.

"Sometime later he came up and hugged me. Every time he sees me, he says, 'Hi! I love you.'"

More Than Anyone Should Bear

Any police officer, firefighter, or emergency medical worker can regale a willing listener with hours of war stories. Bodies pulled from wrecks. Terrible gunshot wounds. The ripping sorrow of a little child's death. Usually, these tales are told with a gallows humor that can only be appreciated by others in the profession. These people who are paid to meet death face to face develop a certain pride in having the grisliest story to tell. One-up-manship is one of the methods they use to cope with the routine horror.

But not in Oklahoma City. The public safety officers certainly talk over and over about what happened. They are still doing so. But it's a bewildered attempt to deal with the enormity of their experience. And there is no gallows humor.

Chaplains comment constantly about the unique attitude of public safety officers to the tragedy. They point to that unique attitude as ample evidence of God's hand in the events. Not totally tongue-in-cheek, a chaplain at ground zero observes, "It would just about take a miracle to subdue your average public safety officer's kick-the-devil-in-the-butt bravado."

The army of chaplains who back these people up agree to a person: What public safety officers found at the site, when it happened and for weeks afterward, is more than a human being ought to have to bear.

Horror

A combination of circumstances made the bombing unique in America and then multiplied its effects. The site and the fate of the victims was horrific beyond description. Shock and disbelief made the horror harder to take. Frustration made it even worse. And public safety officers were called upon to absorb almost the full impact of that combination of feelings and circumstances.

Shock and Disbelief

Ask anyone, civilian or professional responder, for an initial reaction to the news. The same answers kept being repeated:

- "I was shocked. I couldn't believe it! This is Oklahoma, America's heartland. This could not have happened here!" Over and over.
- "I can't imagine anyone doing this. And to *children*!"
- ". . . Nightmare! I keep hoping it's a bad dream."
- "We lost our innocence."

In the immediate aftermath, scores of victims and people who worked at the site would say, "I wasn't really functioning mentally. It was too overwhelming."

The shock and disbelief were emotionally and intellectually numbing. But frustration compounded them.

Frustration

Medical personnel, almost instantly mobilized on disaster alert, were all geared up and ready to treat thousands. *Eager* to treat. Every hour of training and experience in their whole lives was focused on these next few hours; this was the moment of a lifetime for which they had prepared.

But nothing. That first wave of injured, the walking wounded and those few pulled alive from the surface wreckage, flowed into area medical facilities. The second wave never happened. Medical personnel stood around looking at each other, growing more frustrated and volatile by the hour.

Workers on the site who braved great danger to find survivors experienced the same frustration. The hulk was incredibly unstable. Large portions of the shattered building could have come crashing down on workers at any time. No one knew how far and how badly the structural damage extended. That east wall, in particular, seemed to be held up only by the rubble at its base. Still they dived into the wreckage, digging frantically.

They left the dead dangling in order to find the living. They ignored severed limbs to find the person still breathing.

Nothing.

Hours. Nothing.

Jim Strickland, Task Force Leader of the Fairfax County (Virginia) Urban Search and Rescue Task Force, says that his unit, like every other team, were hoping very much to find people alive. "It would have been a great feeling if our Task Force could have saved a life."

To which Oklahoma and the world would reply, *We wish so too, Mr. Strickland. We wish so too.*

Frustration erupted in other ways as well. Emergency workers are trained to save everyone, every time. No matter how tough a situation looks, EMS and other personnel assume they're going to produce a miracle and go for it. That kind of never-give-up attitude has saved many lives. But it takes a heavy, heavy toll on the workers, because they can't save everyone, every time. On this occasion, they could do precious little saving of any sort.

Nor was it a swift rescue effort. So jumbled was the wreckage, clawing through it became a terribly slow process. It would be so easy to shift some bit of crumpled concrete and inadvertently crush a living person trapped underneath it. Hurry the least little bit, and you might kill someone beneath you. Things had to be lifted cautiously, not shoved aside, and the things to be lifted weighed tons.

The miracle is that the work proceeded as quickly as it did.

But all the shock and frustration were secondary to the primary jolt, the unspeakable carnage itself. Day after day, rescuers had to deal with situations not even a horror-movie producer could dream up.

With highly uncharacteristic restraint—a miracle in itself, when you think about it—the world's news media greatly downplayed the grisly nature of the situation and the hideous condition of so many victims. They would tell you that they were sparing the feelings of the victims' families, as if news media are normally sensitive to that.

As a result, few people think about what the public safety officers and the search and rescue teams had to deal with daily. The rescuers insist that only someone on the scene could begin to understand.

Police officer Jay Barnett's experience was typical:

"When the bomb went off, I was in bed sick with the flu. I'd been up all night. I got dressed and went 10-8, which means I was available for duty. After responding on several calls in the area, I came to the scene. As I entered the site at about 10:00 A.M., one of the first things I saw was a torso that I could identify as a woman's torso.

"When I saw a doll's head, I knew there had been a day-care center. I felt sick. This was beyond my worst nightmare. I wanted it to be a dream. Everybody I was coming to had already been located and they were dead. I remember seeing one body, where the face was ripped off. None of this was stuff that I hadn't seen before, but never all in one place. Never this type of carnage. I hope I will never see it again.

"When I saw the picture of a family in the rubble, I kept thinking of all the families. I personalized it."

At the scene during the first minutes, few people if any realized yet the extent of what had happened. The words *dazed* and *numb* occur constantly in narratives. They went into a mechanical mode, furiously conducting the hasty searches that would rescue the living, not really thinking about what was happening there. Many rescuers tell about some sight or sound—such as the doll's head that jolted Jay Barnett—that slapped the rescuer in the face with the enormity of the human tragedy. Not infrequently, these reality checks would occur after the person left the site.

One witness says, "I was doing all right, I thought, until I saw a child standing on a street corner with his mom later that day in another part of the city. Then I just came apart." Just seeing that child in a normal environment, safe and protected by a parent, triggered the pain of seeing innocent children so horribly harmed.

Most witnesses to the scene experienced this grief and sorrow. Jay Barnett remembers a lady who came around 2:00 in the afternoon. She had been to all the hospitals. Her child was in day care. She explained to him that she had already been to all the hospitals and they had told her to come back down to the site because rescue operations were under way. She wanted to know where they were taking people that they were getting out.

"I didn't know what to tell her because they hadn't gotten anyone out," Jay remembers. "I was going to say something to her to the effect that they were still working, but they hadn't gotten anyone out yet at that point. Before I got the words out of my mouth—the look on my face— she understood.

"She started sobbing. She screamed like I have never heard anyone scream. Somebody was there with her. She balled up next to the building and was sobbing. The person with her wrapped their arms around her and picked her up and left. I told them they might be able to get information at the Red Cross. It was pretty helpless.

"Throughout that first day, since there were no reports of dead bodies, people held out hope there wouldn't be any. I had hoped that, until I saw the scene.

"On the way home that night, I cried."

Almost uniformly, witnesses refrained from describing the full horror of what they saw. This silence, partly born of shock and dismay, partly born of confusion and perhaps anger, did nothing to help the rescuers and other public safety officers. Imagine experiencing the most horrible thing you could ever experience, and the world acts as if it did not exist.

Again, here's where the hands-on attitude of the chaplains at ground zero proved to be a splendid blessing for the workers. Because the chaplains were right there lending their help, seeing the sights and smelling the smells that the rescuers had to contend with, they could listen as no one else could.

One anonymous rescuer said, "I'm probably saying more than I ought to, especially since the loss is still so fresh for all those people. We didn't talk about it at the time, mostly for that reason. Partly because we couldn't, I suppose.

"I'm one of the people brought in from outside. By the time I got there, we were beginning to look on it as a retrieval operation instead of a rescue. You know the difference; rescue workers look for survivors. Retrieval personnel don't. We didn't admit it, of course, even to ourselves, but it was starting to look like our only job was digging out bodies.

"Bodies. The walking wounded and the people they dug out alive on that first day weren't messed up real bad, comparatively speaking, not even the lady who lost a leg. Neither were a few of the first corpses they bagged. Oh, sure, some of them lost some parts, but they were relatively intact. They sort of gave everyone the idea that the whole operation was going to be like that. Nasty, but not *too* bad. We were wrong.

"Some of the next-of-kin were upset because they weren't asked to identify the remains by sight. They didn't realize what the remains looked like. There weren't any features you could identify. Jewelry. Wallets. A tag of fabric. That's how they did it. They brought in Clyde Snow, probably the world's best identifier of remains, to help them. Considering what they had to work with, they did a phenomenal job. Just phenomenal.

"So this reporter sticks a mike in my face and asks me, 'How do you manage to keep going back in there, when the work is so gruesome?'

"And even while she's asking that, I'm thinking, *Lady, you can't begin to know the tenth of what gruesome is. We've redefined the term here.* So I say, 'No problem. We're not scraping up people.' (I used exactly those words, *scraping up.*) 'The people are long gone. We're just retrieving the containers they came in.'

"I shrugged and kept it sort of casual and offhand—for effect, you know? But inside, my heart was breaking."

And so were many others.

The Comfort of Debriefing

Psychologists and chaplains on staff kept a close eye out for workers who might need help. Should an officer seem to be having difficulty, they would get him or her off the scene, and sit down to a debriefing session that would take as long as necessary.

Debriefing serves two purposes. One is to garner a body of information about what works and what doesn't so that the next tragedy will be handled even better. The other, more important purpose, is comfort.

The first thing an officer on the line needs is a way of uncorking the experience. Talk it out. Tell the story over and over. Many people who work in this milieu claim that you have to tell your story a minimum of ten times before the comfort and healing grab hold.

One officer, distraught, said, "If only I could get to a live one. All I carried out were dead bodies and pieces. I'm a failure." The debriefer's response was never, "Oh, that's nonsense! You're not a failure!" The debriefer listened. Asked questions. Listened more. Heard repetition upon repetition. Finally, the healing began and the officer worked past pain to a measure of comfort. Providing comfort is never easy.

The public safety departments will take two to three weeks carefully debriefing all their officers.

The Red Cross, Salvation Army, and a number of other agencies responded because that's what they do. They provided immeasurable help and comfort; the statistics don't begin to tell their story. Agencies less well known played important parts as well.

Like just about everyone else, Andy Kidd, an agent for the State's Alchoholic Beverage Laws Enforcement Commission, worked all kinds of jobs, any shift. He came off a detail at 2:00 one morning, having just been serenaded by an excellent choir. He unwound awhile by reading some of the cards children sent and talked to a cluster of other Christian officers there. They talked about the choir, the kids' cards, lots of things.

"There was so much love being focused here," Andy says. "If anyone had asked what God's love felt like, I could define that. You could feel the energy of all the prayers, the words being spoken, the songs being sung. If heaven's anything like this, I'm ready to go."

This kind of love and respect was also shown to the dead.

The Respect Paid to the Dead

One of the rescuers' basic attitudes, which turned out to also be a means of coping, was the respect paid remains, no matter how mangled. An eyewitness provides this account from late on the third day of operations, Saturday the twenty-second:

"Three distinctly different operations were going on. FBI and Secret Service people were searching through file cabinets and the rubble for sensitive information. Everything, every ongoing investigation, every undercover agent, was bared to the world in that rubble. They had to get it.

"The ATF and FBI and others were also investigating the bombing itself. A backhoe operator was gathering debris from the rubble pile and spreading it out on the ground so that agents could sift through it with rakes. They were looking for bomb fragments and any other clues they could use in their investigation. They searched every square inch of rubble. Then a mini-dozer would scoop it up and load it in a dump truck. I understand they searched through it again away from the disaster site.

"And the third was the rescue operation. The rescuers were cooperating with the FBI and the others, of course, but they didn't give a rip about those aspects. They had their own hell to wade through.

"This particular night, they were way up on the pile going after a body that the dogs had alerted them to, somewhere down inside. The New York City Search and Rescue Squad had this one. Once they got closer, they could identify it as one of the special agents with the Drug Enforcement Agency.

"As they started the actual extrication, almost everyone in the inner perimeter, the area within a block of the building, stopped to watch. These New York City pros, total strangers, removed the fallen agent with great care and laid him out on a gurney—a stretcher. They used the same care you'd give a beloved family member. They carried the gurney down to ground level where someone sprayed the body with a decontaminant. Then they slipped him into a black plastic body bag and zipped it shut.

"No one said a word the whole time. The New York City crew and workers from the other agencies lined up to form an honor guard. Eight men gathered around the agent and bowed their heads. You could tell who were Catholics as they crossed themselves, though nobody really noticed, or cared.

"No one broke the silence. They carried the agent out past a line of police officers, U.S. marshals, some military, FBI, DEA, ATF, firefighters, volunteers— everyone. Some saluted; some took their hard hats off and held them over their hearts.

"I know for a fact, grown men cried."

Unique Need

The combination of circumstances, then, drove these volunteers and public servants to the edge of their capabilities—at times, beyond the edge. There is just so much the human mind can absorb. The unique need called for a strength that at times had to be greater than human.

Because they were professionals, the workers were determined to do the job without shirking. When they found themselves lacking the strength to do it alone, they had no choice but to turn to God for that strength. God in response comforted them individually through the chaplains and others who represented Him. And He galvanized community and the world to give them the unique support this unique circumstance required.

Was He there? Ask the workers, even the very first ones on the scene.

But these unique needs and God's response to them provide much more than merely another piece of evidence of God's hand. They tell important things about how God works.

First, God provides spiritual strength directly. It can be felt though not seen. In the aftermath of the blast, public safety officers talk about it a lot, whether they believe in God or not. The worker with the infrared camera illustrates the infusion of that superhuman strength. He could never have gone back to work under his own power, and he knew it.

Second, God sends His servants who have made themselves available to deliver tangible strength in other ways. Human agents. Again, He uses whoever is open to use.

We see then that God's working is not some fuzzy, vaguely defined, sticky-sweet pat on the head from a distant spirit in the clouds. God's help is very personal, a guts-and-glory combination of spiritual and material help, solid reality, palpable in both its spiritual and tangible dimensions.

The servants during the disaster, pushed to the edge, could have functioned with nothing less.

CHAPTER SEVEN

The Miracle of Unity Despite Differences

WHETHER WORKERS BELIEVED IN GOD OR not, all seemed to appreciate the spiritual dimension of Oklahoma City's response. Prayer, usually an irregular act, almost immediately became the normal thing to do. All served capably. All were ministered to.

The logistics of that ministry is a tale in itself.

The Mix of the Secular and the Sacred

First, a bit of background: Most readers are aware that there are a variety of different schools of thought in professional counseling. Advocates of one sort of approach feel that theirs is the best possible for the greatest number of hurting people, even as advocates of a different method tout their own views. Psychology literature abounds in the arguments and defenses.

They do, however, agree on basic tenets. One is that surface solutions are stopgaps at best, and no real improvement will come unless the deep issues are explored and resolved. Another is that you need a lot of specialized training in order to be considered an adequate counselor. A psychotherapist without at least a master's degree (preferably, of course, a doctorate) is a little bit suspect. A third is that these professionals care intensely about the patients they serve; they absolutely abhor the thought of inexperienced or inadequate counselors messing around inside hurting people's heads, and rightly so.

Pastoral counselors—the clergymen and rabbis whom so many members of religious houses turn to automatically—may or may not have any formal training whatsoever in psychological techniques. Many pastoral counselors, in fact, distrust nontheistic psychology as taught at college level and avoid it. Most of them are certain that without God in the equation, counsel is futile. Dig into all the deeper issues you want; your relationship with God is the overriding factor.

In short, many pastoral counselors consider secular counsel to be nothing more than a feeble human attempt to compensate for a divine lack, and therefore doomed from the start. Secular counselors see pastoral counselors as sort of a modern version of witch doctors. It would seem that there is no way peace could bring together these totally divergent positions.

This dichotomy, this wall between disciplines, surfaced early at First Christian Church, the place where family members gathered and waited for word about missing loved ones. A mental health expert (secular side of the wall) from Tulsa, who was an experienced disaster counselor and a veteran of a locally famous tornado tragedy, more or less took over at the center. That was good. He was qualified; he was experienced.

His early plans to help the victims' families seemed to elude pastoral workers.

Meanwhile, pastors were flocking in to help out as chaplains and counselors. It was beginning to look as if they might not be welcomed at the primary sites. By Thursday morning, April 20, the tension was thick enough to ride a horse across.

Into First Christian walked Jack Poe, the Oklahoma City police chaplain. Bradley Yarbrough, pastor at Grace Community Church, took Jack aside. "There may be a problem."

Jack sat down with the others in an organizational meeting. "Folks, I am here by the authority of the mayor's office, and there will be access given to the clergy."

Fine. The secular psychologists agreed. Then they added that, of course, the clerical counselors would have to be screened. "We don't want just anyone walking in. This is a site where we must offer both protection and help." Any clergy taking part would have to be highly qualified, and that included earned degrees in the appropriate field.

Said Jack in effect, "But clerical screening *is* the clergy's job. We'll handle it, not you."

Who would do the screening?

Jack pointed to Brad Yarbrough. "He's in charge."

Thus did Bradley Yarbrough take over organizing the clerical contingent. He was a businessman who felt the call of God strongly enough to quit his full-time business for a full-time pastorate. He possesses no degrees in psychology or counseling. In fact, he does not have a seminary degree. He is most of all a superb organizer obedient to the voice of God. At the time, as it turns out, that's exactly what was needed.

At first, the organization was so complex that counselors met once an hour for assignments. Some made building security their priority, others the rescue workers on-site and the ever-present media. Some worked directly with the medical examiner, in immediate contact with the morgue. Military families had to be served according to armed forces protocols, which differed in important regards from civilian practice. For example, an armed forces chaplain was dispatched to the home of any military family experiencing loss. A number of pastoral counselors worked right there at First Christian.

And then there were the media. Trucks, cameras, and reporters parked in the cement driveway, hungry for any crumb of news or human interest that might fall. Who would serve as media representative and, when necessary, as a buffer for families who didn't want to be bothered by reporters? All those tasks had to be allotted.

Later, as service settled into routine, the meetings were held every two hours. By Friday, an organizational chart was posted and meetings occurred sporadically as needed.

But what about the clergy? Counsel is intensely draining for the counselor. To hold and help a distraught loved one sucks energy out at an unbelievable rate. When a family member pours out his frustration and despair, that frustration and despair become the chaplain's own. There is no distancing oneself in this business. The clergy themselves needed support, succor, a sympathetic ear.

So clergy were assigned to help the clergy. Brad Yarbrough oversaw that aspect himself.

Says Brad of those first organizational hours, "The secular psychologists were absolutely right; screening was necessary. Standards had to be high, if we were to be effective. But what standards? Not merely secular standards. These were going to be godly ministers meeting spiritual needs. They had to be spiritually effective. With God's leading, we developed a strong set of criteria right from the start. As we look at the operation in retrospect, we see that it worked perfectly."

Number one priority for any pastoral counselor had to be integrity. Integrity voiced itself in several ways.

One way was that the minister must be able to respond to the Spirit of God. That's what pastoral counsel was all about. By now, just about everyone realized that the Spirit of God was moving strongly through the whole effort. He was there, and the minister had to be able to respond to His leading.

Another aspect of pastoral integrity was the deliberate abandonment of "churchianity." For a lot of pastors steeped in their denomination, this was very difficult. But the rule was inviolable: No pastor would proselytize for his or her faith or for a specific church. The need was universal; the response must be universal. Roman Catholic, Baptist, Methodist, Nazarene, and many others stood side-by-side offering the same comfort, the same wise help. There was unity in the Spirit and not a hint of denominational division.

A final aspect of integrity cannot be expressed clearly in words. Some call it "gifting." It is the capacity to help and it cannot be faked. Only those involved in full-time ministry in a local congregation were to work with the families.

Says Brad, "There were times when it was really tough, because we turned people away. Turning away incompetents is not tough. Turning away dedicated Christians is. It wasn't that they weren't any good. They certainly were. It was just that they didn't meet the particular requirement we needed in that situation."

As the number two priority, those who would serve had to really follow the Lord's lead instead of kiting off on their own. This was much easier said than done.

Brad Yarbrough himself knew how difficult this might be: "I had always thought that the most meaningful ministry, perhaps the only meaningful ministry, was preaching the gospel and leading people into a saving relationship with Jesus Christ. In this situation, I suddenly found myself being 'only' a vessel of compassion and mercy. I wasn't leading people to Jesus through teaching or preaching. I considered myself as the hand of the Lord, reaching out with a tender touch. I really had to wrestle in prayer with the possibility that I had succumbed to an ugly, nearly unacceptable compromise.

"Aren't we supposed to remind people to repent? Aren't we supposed to be constantly bent upon leading them to Christ? After all, the soul without Christ dies!

"These issues plagued my mind. I brought it up to the other pastors and the message became clear: We were the vessels of His compassion just now.

That was all, and that was sufficient. That's where He wanted us.

"We were wearing the compassion and love of God as though it were a garment. Any and every denomination, we were all wearing the same garment. The families saw it and they were embracing us. They had a deep, deep need that only God in His compassion could meet. His face of love shaped our countenance. These hurting people were requesting our prayers. They were reaching out for the love they saw in us. People would tell us, 'I see God in your face.'

"It's hard to put into words. Profound things always are. I was aware that I was expressing a level of compassion I had never manifested before. It wasn't me. It was God through me.

"Another pastor put the capper on it for me. 'Brad, do you remember Romans 2:4? It is the loving kindness of the Lord that leads to repentance.'

"I no longer consider the expression of God's love and compassion to be any sort of compromise at all."

And So the Wall Came Down

Forced into close proximity to the secular counselors (a few of the pastors coming into direct contact with counselors of modern psychology for the first time ever), the clergy gained an appreciation—and more importantly, a solid respect—for those who had a sincere desire to use their training to help others.

In the eyes of the secular counselors, the image of the proselytizing witch doctor began to fade. These clerical people really did possess an integrity transcending personal agendas. They delivered spiritual insight that helped the hurting heart.

As mutual distrust dissolved, the wall weakened and tumbled. Overwhelmed by the enormity of what they were facing, some of the secular counselors came to the clergy for prayer. Quietly, one day when no one was noticing, "either-or" became "both."

To date, the Red Cross, a secular humanitarian organization, has not used religious resources at disaster scenes. Based upon the experience in Oklahoma City, their reservations about doing so have dissolved to a large extent. They are now meeting with clerical veterans of the Murrah bombing to work out ways in which spiritual needs might be met in future disasters.

The Miracle Is Recognized

While family members waited, gifts of flowers, food, and drink poured in. The material gifts told these hurting people that other people cared. The spiritual and psychological support there told them that people right here cared. The First Christian Church became, in the words of the facility's supervisor, a warm nest for hurting people.

"It was amazing," said one of the counselors. "I remember an older couple, whose daughter was missing. They came in for hours on the second day. Within another day or so, they were staying there just about all the time, loath to go home. They became part of a splendid, splendid support group.

"Finally they received word that the woman's body had been identified. The waiting was over. We expected them to just sort of disappear. They didn't. They stayed, and kept returning, even though they knew for sure that it was over. So, as tactfully as I could, I asked them why.

"The mother replied, 'For right now, this is our family. This is where the caring is. It's comforting here.' She hesitated a moment. 'And here is where we can do some good comforting others.'"

Joann Thompson, whose husband, Mike, died, called First Christian Church a refuge. "We [Joann and her sons] had the feeling we never wanted to leave it."

At the site, workers received whatever comfort they needed. In the hospitals, chaplains, family members, and other comforters abounded. When young day-care victim Christopher Nguyen was released, a nurse commented, "He didn't just have his parents coming in to comfort him. His whole family showed up."

The Miracle Is Articulated

The Red Cross received major attention in media descriptions of the scene, of course. They played a crucial role, as they always do. But as the first news stories danced around the world via satellite and wire, local pastors noticed that no mention was made of the powerful spiritual nature of people's responses.

All those reporters hanging around First Christian Church seemed to want only the sensational human interest stuff they figured would appeal to a largely secular audience. If they felt the pervasive spirit of God everyone else was feeling, they were keeping it to themselves.

Where was the story about the way the churches leaped into the relief effort and how deeply they became instantly involved? The story about the strong presence of the chaplains and their role? The story about the comfort people were taking in the Spirit of God? The outside world was not adequately seeing God at work.

Brad Yarbrough brought the point up with the media coordinator. "The spiritual dimension of this effort is palpable. How do we tell people what God is doing here, and how much a part of the relief effort prayer has become?"

"Not a problem. We'll take you down to the press conferences. You tell them."

It sounded easy. But everyone knows, media reporters aren't interested in reporting soft news like religious responses. They want the hard stuff.

Not this time. Hungry for stories, the reporters saw column inches and on-camera minutes in the amazing spiritual response of Oklahoma City to its greatest tragedy. Local religious leaders were soon getting interviews from all over the country.

Under the headline, "A Shaken City, Ever Devoted, Turns to God," the Sunday, April 30, *New York Times* ran pictures as well as stories of God at work. An article out of Syracuse, New York, quoted local OKC clergy. CNN reported to the world the work that God was doing among the families.

You had to be deaf, dumb, and blind to miss the message.

Ministers Also Take the Front Line

Thursday morning, April 20, as soon as some of those organizational knots were unraveled and straightened out at First Christian, Brad Yarbrough and others went down to the site. "It was a terrible, horrible sight," says Yarbrough. "Just terrible. There were moments of total shock as I viewed the devastation.

"I walked up to an Oklahoma City police detective who had just come out of the ruined building. I began a conversation with him. Then I asked, 'May I pray for you?'

"He bowed his head and we prayed. We both cried.

"Later I asked a friend if he knew that detective.

"His reply: 'I do, and I can't believe he let you pray with him. That's not his lifestyle. He's not a religious man.'

"He was then. And that is pretty much the story of what went on down there. Everyone was turning to God because God was pouring Himself out. The hovering Spirit of God was upon the whole scene."

Rescue workers took to the spiritual ministry the way a dog laps water. During the first hours, the chaplains would help with whatever dirty work needed to be done. As they served in that way, they watched the workers around them. If someone appeared dazed or overcome by emotion, a chaplain would move in beside with a gentle, "How are you doing?"

Everyone on-site had to wear a hard hat or the equivalent (riot helmet or fire helmet, for instance). Chaplains' hard hats were usually marked with a cross. The chaplains who waded into the jaws of destruction with the search and rescue units, though, didn't even look like male or female.

"All they could see were your eyes," recalls Tim Jones of Tulakes Baptist Church. Anyone who entered the ruin had to wear a mask or respirator to protect against dust (crystalline dust can cause pneumonia by irritating lungs), inhaled dirt, and quite possibly toxic fumes. The mask plus the hard hat just about blotted out facial features. "Your eyes had to be loving and kind."

Within two nights, rescue workers knew who the chaplains were, mask or no mask. The chaplains no longer had to initiate contact; the workers sought them out when they needed something.

Some workers had special needs apart from the obvious ones. For example, to a person outside the Roman Catholic faith, "The Blessing," "Extreme Unction," and "Commendation of the Dead" don't mean a whole lot. To practicing Catholics they mean the world. Father Joe Meinhart, a chaplain from Bishop McGuinness High School, made sure that his services were received when they were needed. His services were surely needed April 19. Immediately Father Joe coordinated a twenty-four-hour schedule of Catholic priests to serve on-site, fulfilling those special needs.

Father Joe didn't limit himself to the needs of Catholics; nobody serving as chaplains and pastoral counselors limited themselves in any way. He'd pray with anybody and bless anyone who required it. Pretty soon the relationship between rescuers and chaplains took on a symbiotic quality—mutual support and benefit rather than benefits pouring in one direction only.

Workers found a Marine captain, Randy Guzman, seated at his desk, dead, still under a pile of rubble eight feet high. They had dug down through the top to reach him and ascertain his condition. Father Joe needed to be up there to give the Commendation of the Dead. Not a problem. The workers built a platform in order to reach the body and boosted Father Meinhart onto it. Then they positioned him so that he could be next to the body in order to pray for him.

It took the workers five hours to extricate the body intact. The captain was then placed on the same board used to lift the father, and then lowered to a gurney and handed over to a Marine honor guard.

There was a point in the grueling, relentless operation when one minister, Tim Jones, asked himself why he kept coming back. Then he answered his own question: "I kept coming back because the guys on the rescue teams kept telling us, 'Hey, thanks for being here.' Part of our task was to be a spiritual presence, to represent God in that building."

Father Meinhart echoes that feeling. "Ours was a ministry of presence. We were there to let the people know that while this looks like a victory of death over life, it is actually a victory of life over death."

<u>Part Three:</u>

Healing in the Heartland

CHAPTER EIGHT

Lessons from the Perimeter

TEN MINUTES AFTER THE BOMB WENT off, Oklahoma Highway Patrol trooper Scott Watkins and others had established a perimeter around the north side of the building. "We were here within minutes. We had to send the right people into the area and keep curiosity seekers out of the area."

It sounds so simple. It could hardly have been more difficult or complex.

A perimeter at its simplest is that yellow police line—DO-NOT-CROSS plastic ribbon you sometimes find at a scene, stretched out, and tied or duct-taped to whatever object might be handy—a tree, a porch post, a fire hydrant. Orange traffic cones help, and every emergency vehicle carries them.

The perimeter at the Murrah building started out as tape, which was quickly replaced with pipe-and-wire fencing units. It enclosed the destroyed north side first, where the prospect of danger and trouble loomed greatest. A while later, the first phase of the hasty search completed and the walking wounded pretty well taken care of, the south side was closed off. To protect the debris that could be evidence about the bomb and bomber, law enforcement officials closed down the whole block.

The physical boundaries were the least of it. From the first moment, public safety officers were nearly swamped by the enormity of the situation. Emotional barriers formed instantly. People in public safety agencies are good at forming barriers; they do it without trying. Particularly on this occasion, block-outs to protect emotions were the only way to prevent the horror from collapsing officers' ability to do the job.

Every officer who responded in those first minutes reports, "I was dazed. On hold. I had to do my job without thinking; I couldn't think." Training and experience kicked in automatically, and all the officers there performed their duties quickly and ably, but it wasn't because they thoughtfully worked out a plan of action first.

Paramedic Mike McElroy describes it: "Maybe three hundred walking wounded wandering around. Shattered glass, layers of shattered glass all over.

everywhere. It numbed you. Even before you saw the building gutted, it numbed you.

"I've been a paramedic for twenty-one years. I was on my way to work when I heard the bomb. Before I was paged, I headed toward the explosion.

"The emergency response to the scene in the first moments arrived—well, in the first moments. A fire station was only a couple of blocks away. A police station was five blocks away or so. Several ambulances happened to be rolling already in the area, so we just diverted and headed for the smoke. And several hospitals were pretty close. So we were all right there.

"I'm constantly amazed how well it all meshed together, from the very first. There was a lot of yelling and running around, but it was people trying to do more than was humanly possible; it wasn't random. It was a real complex operation."

Police officers' duties were complex also. While firefighters dug frantically, police officers took part in the initial hasty search for survivors, assisted wounded, established safe triage areas and directed incoming medical personnel, kept the merely curious out of the way, provided comfort to those uncertain about loved ones, handled traffic and granted access to the emergency vehicles, and last but not least, maintained the integrity of the crime scene.

Maintaining the integrity of the crime scene was a massive pain in the neck. From a forensics investigator's perspective, every criminal should victimize one person at a time when only those two are in a room. Only one investigating officer enters that room (or, even better, none at all) and then the forensics team comes in and finds all sorts of solid, incriminating micro-evidence untainted by extraneous events and other people. It never ever happens that way, and it certainly did not at the Murrah building.

A wave of bystanders flowed up into that ruined north side immediately, answering the cries of trapped people, digging recklessly through the debris. So much for a virgin crime scene—and yet no one would have had it any other way. Hundreds of public safety personnel and medical people swarmed in, and no one would have had that any other way, either. The Secret Service, ATF, FBI, DEA, and U.S. marshals, all housed in the building, rushed their own investigators and agents to the scene, partly to help with the rescue effort, partly to recover sensitive material.

In spite of all, order rose above chaos quickly. The FBI took over as the investigating agency in control. The Federal Emergency Management Agency stepped in within hours to coordinate rescue efforts and to mesh them with the FBI's efforts to investigate the bombing for what it was—a mass murder.

They established two perimeters. The Oklahoma Highway Patrol, police, and the Oklahoma National Guard secured an outer one which some people might enter, with permission. U.S. marshals and Oklahoma City police secured the inner perimeter. For that one, you needed a badge to get through, along with a paper issued by the agency with whom you either worked or volunteered. To get that badge, you had to explain your purpose to an FBI agent in charge. The color of your badge determined which perimeter you would be allowed to enter.

Says one firefighter, "That's the first time since grade school that I needed a note from home just to go to the bathroom."

A chaplain explains about pastors who worked the inner perimeter: "Although chaplains working with the bereaved and the anxious at First Christian Church and elsewhere might switch assignments, only a few chaplains worked with rescuers inside the inner perimeter, and they kept the same job all through the weeks. There are several reasons. Most important, probably, is that the rescuers came to know us well and we knew them. Barriers fell aside, you see. A reason almost as important is that the investigators didn't want to keep memorizing a lot of new faces and wondering, 'Should this guy be in here or not?' It was primarily a security situation."

What Went on at the Perimeter

The vast majority of people who came to see, and there were tens of thousands as the work dragged on, respected that chain-link fencing. Children pushed their noses through the mesh holes, as children must do, to get a view two inches closer. Parents held their preschoolers and pointed out what was happening, hoping against hope that these little children would see and remember for a lifetime.

Most simply stood by the fence and watched in silence. Although such fences usually hold back what can only be called a carnival atmosphere, there was nonesuch at the site. People who came used the words *reverence* and *respect* to describe the atmosphere which prevailed.

Most. There's always the clown who flouts the rules. One of the least compelling reasons for security, one nobody talked about, was the law enforcement officer's intense, natural displeasure with gate crashers—people who delight in wangling themselves into places they shouldn't be. Arrest and a nominal fine awaited anyone who transgressed. Dedicated gate crashers don't sweat that stuff.

A firefighter described two young men who donned the gear of firefighters and claimed they were from Springfield, Missouri. They got themselves assigned to a rescue group and rode up in the crane with others to about the third or fourth floor.

The tragedy was hours old; gate crashers work fast. The firefighter noticed one of them taking snapshots and the other calling on a cellular, telling someone, "Hey, I'm on top of the pile!"

The firefighter did not yell. He did not rage. In charge of the scene, he quietly directed those two young men to stand over there—beneath a bus-sized chunk of hanging concrete that could go at any moment. They were to tell him if it moved. The shift ended and the crane returned to take workers back to ground zero. The fellows disappeared instantly.

Fortunately, people like that were rare indeed. This is not to say that the fence was merely a barrier behind which to stand. It was used and used well. That cold, unrelenting, steel wire wall said by its very appearance "ugliness." Instead it became an instrument for beauty, for expression, and even for healing.

For all the hundreds of workers and the army of volunteers in the background who supported them, thousands were left with no way to express or release their feelings. Over and over:

- "I want to do something!"
- "Isn't there *anything* I can do?"
- "What can I do?"

Too often, the response had to be, "Nothing at this time. Sorry."

Mourning Oklahomans turned to that fence.

From the beginning, people like Cyndy McGarr, who wrote the volunteer's prayer out on butcher paper and hung it on the fence, used it to display their thoughts. Signs offered encouragement and God's blessings on those who worked inside the perimeter and those who had lost loved ones.

The perimeter fence, particularly the fence at the corner of Sixth and Hudson, became a sort of shrine to the fallen and the workers. Other shrinelike sites developed. People hung banners and laced long-stemmed roses into the fence netting. Wreaths went up. So many flowers and teddy bears poured in that workers strung up a plastic tarp to provide a sheltered area. At another site, the Oklahoma flag stood watch over a mountain of fragile beauty—flowers and wreaths, bows and bears galore. Elaborate floral arrangements or a single bud out of the backyard garden said, "I care. I can't do much else, but I can do this."

Jack Poe, the Oklahoma City police chaplain, tells of one incident at the fence: "About 8:00 one evening, a little boy walked up to one of these memorabilia locations and laid down a twenty-dollar bill. One of our police officers asked him to take it back and not let money just lie there. Almost instantly, a couple of other people passing by put down more money. Before our officers could stop it and turn folks around, a hundred and forty-nine dollars were down in the street.

"Our people put it in a sealed evidence envelope. What else can you do with it?"

At no time has anyone, to any person's knowledge, ever taken something from the fences or shrines. Quite probably, the money would have been as safe on the street as it was in the evidence bag. It was that kind of a time.

As the days crawled by, the fence became increasingly festooned with these material expressions and no one took them away. They greatly softened the harsh meaning of that cold wire mesh and muted its criminal overtones.

Lessons from the Perimeter

A rescue worker, when the search was suspended prior to the implosion, said: "I've seen it all. Most of it I've experienced in person. So when I see something on TV that shows how warped people can be, it doesn't surprise me. I'm thinking of when an elevated train derailed and perfectly healthy people from off the street started climbing up into the wreck so that they could collect damages.

"Everyone by now has heard how businesses at some other disaster sites would rip off the rescue teams by charging enough money for food and other needs to put braces on your kid's teeth. Or when scumbags stole equipment from the teams and then offered to sell it back to them.

"I wasn't expecting much more when we got to Oklahoma City. I hadn't seen anything until then. *Now* I've seen it all.

"Everyone has heard about the royal reception the out-of-towners got, with mints on the pillows and all that. It's all true. Whatever we needed, *poof!* there it was. Nothing ever happened like that before.

"But there's more. I could even say *infinitely* more. They supplied us with the one thing we'd never gotten before, the thing we needed most of all. I don't even have a word for it. *Debriefing* is too cold. *Support* is too vague. *Nurturing,* I guess. They gave it to us through prayer—they were dropping by to pray for us and with us all the time—and spiritual things like church choirs that would come by to sing for us. I never in my life had bothered with prayer before, and all of a sudden, I discovered I wanted it.

"Most of all, there were enough chaplains and other sympathetic, listening ears that when we came off a shift we could unload. Even in the middle of a shift, for that matter.

"You don't know how important that is. You can't.

"Let me give you an example. Police officers build a tall, tight wall around themselves. Cops band together and all their friends are cops, and they marry cops, and they give birth to cops. Retired cops have a real high suicide rate because they can't exist outside that circle of cops, and when they retire they find themselves outside

The blast lifted the center portions of the upper floors and sheared their moorings. Support gone, these floors ripped loose and freefell onto the first two floors. As rescuers combed the debris on the ground, other workers used cranes and bare hands to clear hanging wreckage that was likely to fall.

"I saw black smoke rising from downtown," claim many, many witnesses who were miles away. The bomb-ripped buildings themselves put up no smoke whatever. It came from burning cars, as in this parking lot across the street from the blast.

The image of the gutted Murrah building will remain one of America's memories forever. But many other buildings were destroyed or damaged past salvaging. Two persons were killed here in the flattened Athenian restaurant and two others died in the Water Resources building beyond.

Within minutes, every child from the day-care center in the YMCA building across the street was out of the wreckage and cradled in the arms of an adult.

Volunteers, police, and firefighters attended hundreds of battered survivors who made it out to the streets, not just from the Murrah building but from all the others around. Flying glass shards dealt the most injury to the walking wounded.

Glass lacerations cause severe bleeding and many victims lost enormous quantities of blood. Swamped with donors, most blood centers asked for type O only on that first day, for O can be given to nearly anyone. The person attended at this scene survived.

In that first hour, whether injured or not, the survivors who fled the ruined buildings sat nearly silent, as in a daze.

Flowers, teddy bears, and other gifts poured in. Single flowers were laced into the cyclone fence of the outer perimeter. Homegrown roses spoke the same message as did elaborate arrangements. And everywhere, the word *bless*.

The north face on the east side. As floors were cleared, the flags went up—many from the states that provided rescue units. The girderlike structure attached to the building is a construction elevator.

This area near ground zero became a shrine to those lost and to those working so doggedly. For many it became holy ground.

A closeup shot of the work on one floor of the building.

Governor Keating addresses Oklahoma City and the world at a memorial held on site a week after the blast. Chaplains, Mayor Ron Norick, and Cathy Keating stand behind him.

This view, taken from above, shows how deeply the bomb gouged the building. At the implosion the center buckled as the walls collapsed toward the middle, leaving a huge mound of rubble.

Thank You For All You Have Done

May God Bless And Protect You

Federal Aviation Administration   Fleet Modernization Staff

Of all the factors that set Oklahoma City's response apart from others, perhaps the most obvious was the pervasive atmosphere of gratitude to those who worked so persistently.

the wall. You leave the service, no matter why, and suddenly you're nothing. That's how high the wall is. That all comes because only working cops can understand what working cops go through.

"It's the same with the fire department or search and rescue, though to a lesser extent. No one but us knows what we're seeing and what we have to go through to do the job. I think another reason to put up the wall is to protect yourself from all the dumb comments and questions civilians ask. That's part of it at least.

"Until Oklahoma City, we didn't have anyone besides us who understood. Who would listen, really listen, while you dump. And sympathize. The chaplains provided that. You see, they were right there beside us, seeing the same stuff we did and once in a while even helping out. They knew the worst. In other words, we could let them inside the wall, at least a little way.

"Not even debriefing and talking it out was enough this time. We discovered that we needed spiritual hands to hold us when we came off a shift. They gave us that too.

"A lot of so-called sophisticated people sneer at the phrase 'Bible Belt.' They better never do that where I can hear."

The Protection of a Perimeter

The perimeter, which emergency services and public safety people put up around themselves, protected them from the full horror of the job. It protected them from the callous curious, the "tourist" type people outside the perimeter who gawked with morbid fascination. The rescuer's comment about protection from ignorance is right on. Thoughtless cracks and flippant remarks by people who don't understand can hurt. So the officers let them bounce off that wall. They don't allow those people to see what's really going on inside.

Perimeters inside people are like the perimeters around the Murrah building in so many ways. Many people, in fact, maintain two sanctums, inner and outer. Sometimes a spouse or good friend can enter the outer area to get a closer look. The inner fence remains closed. It may be that not even the person who owns the walls knows what's in the deepest part.

From the outside, the idle curious are permitted to see only what the protected person, the real person behind the perimeter, wants them to see. Often it's not what is actually there.

"We'd make sure," says a search and rescue worker, "that the body was bagged as quickly as possible. We didn't want the media with their long-range lenses taking morbid pictures. When all that was left for them to see was another black plastic bag, that's when we'd put it on the board and carry it out."

Workers in emergency services as well as a lot of private citizens affected by the tragedy desperately tried to keep up a false front. What they wanted the public to see and what was really happening inside were two completely different things. The perimeter kept that false appearance secure.

All the nasty stuff was tucked away from innocent eyes inside the perimeter. And that was just as well.

"I've seen a lot of carnage," Jay Barnett reflects, "but never like that. Not all that." The carnage got to the officers; imagine its effect on the people *not* accustomed to that sort of thing. The perimeter shielded many from the unspeakable realities inside.

Similarly, the nasty stuff inside people is instinctively walled away, in workers and others alike, lest it become too much to bear. That presents a big problem.

The problem is people's natural resistance to gate crashers. Unwanted guests, to put it euphemistically, grate upon the nerves and the psyche. We all protect our inner barriers against gate crashers, the people we don't trust enough to let in there, the people who might not understand, the people who might hurt more than help, the people who might tramp upon our fragile egos and feelings.

Although all people erect barriers against the gawkers to some extent, public safety and emergency services workers have honed barriers to a fine art. They've got them wired together solidly enough that nothing is going to get through. The barriers protect, but they also keep the healing out.

At ground zero, people entered the perimeters in order to clean up the site, remove the decaying bodies, and eventually to implode the building, closing the chapter. Getting inside the perimeters of people is not nearly so easy. Chaplains, pastors, psychologists, and therapists yearn to find a way in there and help clean up. The perimeters keep them at bay. Unless the grieving, hurting owner of that perimeter opens a gate, relief cannot enter.

Mike McElroy, the paramedic, understood at first hand the needs of emergency and public safety workers, the needs of all those thousands of others affected by the incident, and by extension the needs of any person undergoing traumatic loss. His pastor, Reverend Robert Wise, worked the morgue on the first day of the bombing; he understood every bit as well. At Mike's instigation and with his help, Robert Wise conducted a Healing of Memories service for the emergency medical services personnel a few days after the blast.

The fact that the rite was specifically for the emergency medical services workers helped open a gate. *This is for our own.* A part of the service was the expected religious observation. A small part. A large part employed techniques for dealing with traumatic memories. They and other techniques are designed specifically to help the gates swing wide, that healers may get in.

Let's explore some of those methods in better detail.

CHAPTER NINE

Steps to Healing— Salving the Wound

JOE WILLIAMS, DIRECTOR OF CHAPLAINCY, Baptist General Convention of Oklahoma and chaplain of the Oklahoma division of the FBI— day one at ground zero: "The first frenzy of action was about over and we were all waiting for that second wave of victims, the one that never came. I was walking near the site when I saw a deputy sheriff approaching. I've known him for several years. He was holding his arms in front of him as if he were carrying something.

"The arms were empty. I called his name and he altered direction to come over to me. His face was a blank stare.

"'Where are you going?' I asked.

"'I just want to get away from the building.' He stood there a few moments and gradually seemed to melt a bit. 'I just carried a baby out of there without a head.'"

The Damage Toll

Joe and the officer held each other awhile. They sat down on the curb and cried. Then the officer used Joe's cellular to call his wife. Later, in debriefing, he talked about how much the baby reminded him of his granddaughter. That officer is what we call a *secondary victim*.

News accounts, and no doubt history books to come, claim there were 168 victims of the Alfred P. Murrah bombing. That's not true. Certainly, one counts as victims the 168 whom we know died as a direct result of the bomb. Over 600, in the Murrah building and elsewhere, suffered nonfatal injury. They too were victims. A few experienced the bombing in that building or elsewhere but escaped relatively unscathed. They were victims also. But that's just the beginning of the count.

Some say that, on the average, each person has about four or five others whom that person could claim as close family, another four or five close friends, and three hundred casual friends and family—people who are well known but not particularly close (the folks you send a Christmas card to but don't hear much from otherwise). Based on that as a very rough guess, we might say that your average person enjoys real closeness to about ten people.

That's 1,680 persons stricken by grief at the loss of a close friend or relative. They are secondary victims.

On the day of the bombing, 173 were hospitalized at least briefly. That's 1,730 loved ones affected. Deeply affected were the close friends and family members who stood vigil at the bedsides of the severely injured, particularly the children.

That's the tip of the iceberg. Unseen beneath the water, were the thousands of workers directly involved. They either took an active part in the recovery effort or worked the scene in such a way that they were party to the danger of those first days before the ruin was stabilized, and to the horror of the whole operation. From past experience with other tragedies, we know that we must call them secondary victims as well.

Joe's police officer friend is a perfect example. He was traumatized, by which we mean that terrible recollections are seared on his memory and he is going to be a long time getting over the horror he experienced. Over the next weeks, he, like so many others, would work various details at the site. Many of the memories thrust upon him, further injuring the psychological injury, would add to the trauma.

Before he or she retires, your average highway patrol trooper will see a few dozen really bad accidents and hundreds of others. Those really bad accidents will haunt the memory. Now picture a hundred terrible deaths even worse than the worst traffic accident. That's what the workers at the Murrah building dealt with.

All too often, adverse reactions to traumatic events of this sort erupt years after the fact. The men and women suffering these reactions seem to be getting by without problems at the time of the incident. People around them smile and nod and say, "They're handling it just fine." The persons themselves insist, "No problem. I've got it under control."

The trouble comes later. That trouble—irritability, agitation, short-term memory loss, insomnia, other problems—will have a negative impact upon the ten people close to each of these men and women and alienate many others. The trouble has a name: *post-traumatic stress disorder*. But not just people directly involved are affected.

When KQCV/KNTL asked listeners for stories about the bombing, we received a plethora of poems and narratives. Without exception, these submissions are emotion-packed, heart-wrenching. And yet, few of the persons responding had any actual part whatever in the tragedy. A great majority of the prose stories followed this pattern:

- "I was going about the business of the day."
- "A boom rattled the house." If the respondent for some reason failed to hear the boom, or nothing rattled, there was a detailed explanation why not, as if hearing the explosion were an important prerequisite.
- "I turned on the TV and saw what occurred. I was stunned. That couldn't happen here in Oklahoma!"
- "I prayed for all the people involved and asked the Lord what I should do. The Lord told me to continue with the day."

If these essays are any indication, continuing with the day and being unable to take part directly was *nearly* as traumatic as going down there. Incidentally, may we pause to again thank all these people who so generously gave time and effort to tell us their experiences. As a side benefit, the stories we received are extremely valuable as a historical record of an event unique in American history. They will become increasingly valuable in years to come (think what we would give for a record like this of citizens' responses to other catastrophic events in history!).

But some of the letters and stories tell us unsettling things about the reaction of the noninvolved person. Even that person, who was not working on the scene or even present downtown, was shocked by the events. Revulsion is a common theme. Shock and revulsion equal trauma. With numerous exceptions, of course, that person felt extremely guilty for not doing more. In some cases (reading between the lines here), the person felt guilty for not being one of the victims. Over and over, the letters tell us that people not directly involved in the event were very deeply affected.

And the children of Oklahoma! Indeed, children all over America. No one knows what the effects of all this will be upon the children. Hundreds and hundreds of letters and drawings from children poured into Oklahoma City; no doubt they were a tiny portion of the total number of poems and drawings made. Letters from local children and from children a thousand miles away carried the same level of emotional intensity. Distance meant absolutely nothing when children were feeling the effects.

"It's strange, and very telling." A psychologist was looking at the expressive works of small children, a few days after the bombing. "The drawing will show sunshine and flowers and trees. Bright, cheery things. But no people. Sometimes, if they're making a drawing to send to someone else, they'll draw themselves, but that's in the nature of a signature. No people.

"They try to process what they've seen and what they're feeling, and they can't. There's never been a model; there's never been anything like it that they can use as a start to help them work it out."

Researchers are beginning to see that small children are far more adversely affected by what they hear and see, particularly on television, than people previously thought. Are kids resilient enough to blow this off, or are they going to suffer the same post-traumatic problems the adults do? If so, their symptoms will probably differ from adults'. Will we be sharp enough to recognize them early enough to treat the children effectively?

Mental health professionals are bracing for an epidemic of psychological problems four or five years from now, when suppressed anger, confusion, and depression begin to take a toll. They believe they will see a massive rise in cases of post-traumatic stress disorder.

The Affect of Post-Traumatic Stress

You hear about post-traumatic stress in reference to Vietnam vets. Divorce, aimlessness, and suicide marked that whole generation. But is it such a terrible thing for emergency workers? It certainly is, and that point came home tragically in April of 1995.

The story began in 1987 and everybody's heard it. Baby Jessica fell down a well, and Robert O'Donnell was one of those who saved her. For a few months, O'Donnell enjoyed celebrity status. But the adrenaline wore off quickly; the attention and fame disappeared just as fast. Four years later he divorced. He asked his fire department for treatment for post-traumatic stress. The treatment was not offered. Accused of drug misuse, he refused to submit to a urinalysis and resigned from the department. He drifted aimlessly from job to job. His restlessness ended when he took his own life in April, seven-and a-half years after that moment in the rescue shaft when his life changed.

Ironically, his tale, under the caption "Tragedy," appeared in the same issue of *People*, May 15, 1995, that made the Oklahoma City tragedy its cover story.

Anything we can do to cleanse and heal now, while the wound is fresh, will pay big dividends down the road a ways. For that reason, counselors and chaplains took great care to minister as fully as they could in the field to both workers and other citizens alike. Their work began when the wound was ripped open and continues even yet.

Getting Past the First Jolt

One rescuer at ground zero said: "I'm not religious. I figure if God exists, I leave Him alone and He leaves me alone, and we get along. But it impressed me, the care and consideration chaplains treated the dead with.

"During the first days, there were several bodies where we could pry part of the rubble apart, but because of something—a slab or a steel beam—we couldn't free up a limb or two. So they'd bring in amputation instruments and we'd take out most of the remains. The rest we got later. That way, they could go about making an identification before the body disintegrated much.

"What really impressed me, whether it was a body or just a part, was that they treated it with reverence. There was always both a priest and a protestant available as bodies were brought out. The priest would do his mumbly thing and the protestant would pray. I figured it was overkill, you know?

"Then I realized. Most of the time you couldn't tell much about the remains, so they were covering all the bases, you might say. There might be some next of kin saying, 'Father, did my loved one get the right send-off?'—however they phrase it. And either the father or the pastor could say, 'Yes he did.' I really respect the way they honored each other's beliefs.

"We were talking about all this one night when we got off a shift. You'd be surprised the things we'd talk about off shift. Silly stuff, a lot of silly stuff. But also deep stuff. Trying to make sense out of it and never quite doing it.

"Our tech supervisor is an ex-seminary student. He explained the different beliefs of those like the Catholics and the Episcopalians and the Baptists.

"I said the differences didn't sound big enough to be worth fighting over. And he says, 'If it's important to somebody, it's important. So they're being very careful that the important stuff gets done. Besides, when something that's important to somebody is done the way they want it, it helps with the grieving process years down the road.'

"Then he told how when his grandfather died, his father put a penny on each of Grandpop's closed eyelids. It was an old country custom and it made his grandmother feel better. She was afraid her husband would have a rough time getting into heaven unless his son put those pennies there. Now she could get on with the grieving.'

"Okay, so it sounded goofy to me. But this was an old lady who grew up with that belief, and she just suffered a traumatic loss. Who am I to say the pennies wouldn't help the grandfather? And what does it matter? They certainly helped her."

They helped her. The priests and pastors performed appropriate rites for the deceased to accomplish two benefits. One was for the deceased. The other was for the living. Their ministry was as much to the living as the dead, and they wanted desperately to help ease the survivors' way. The more *T*'s they crossed, the more *I*'s they dotted, the easier it would be for the people who depended upon them to cover all the bases.

Counselors wanted to ease immediate suffering, but always at the back of their minds, shadows of the future played. The ministry, by which we mean both secular and spiritual counsel, took several forms in about this order:

1. As we already mentioned debriefing was conducted at the time—discussing, analyzing, talking, talking, talking. The bereaved were given opportunity for counsel from the beginning through now, with special emphasis placed on counseling as they waited, helpless, and when they received definite word about their loved ones.

2. Vigils, worship services, prayer meetings and services, and candlelight services were held at a number of churches, synagogues, and other worship sites nightly or nearly so. Any person who felt the need for a formal service could usually find one when he or she needed it. It goes without saying that these services were not just for the people. They were primarily a connection to God, with love flowing in both directions. These were in addition to regularly scheduled services of worship.

3. A service of Healing of Memories was conducted just for the emergency medical personnel.

4. An Evening of Encouragement, featuring singer Sandi Patti, who was born in Oklahoma

City and whose father co-pastored a church there, comedian/singer Mark Lowry, and author Max Lucado, was aimed at all those persons involved in the effort. Not only a source of encouragement, it was also an important release which allowed the bereaved and anxious the permission to laugh a little, to enjoy life a bit in the midst of the tragedy. It did not reduce the tragedy in any way. It made it bearable.

5. A memorial service at the State Fairgrounds featured Pastor Billy Graham as a speaker. President Clinton and his family attended as did others known throughout the country. This service, while memorializing the lost, also offered support and encouragement on a national scale. Oklahoma City's pain had become America's pain: "Oklahoma City, you are hurting, but you are not alone."

6. On Wednesday, April 26, one week after the bombing, at exactly 9:02 A.M., a service was conducted at the site, with the governor of Oklahoma, the city mayor, and others. The hulk of the Murrah building glowering behind them, chaplains and officials offered support and prayer. For this service, the people directly affected—survivors, workers, and bereaved—entered the perimeter, most for the

first time since that dreadful day, and gathered in close to the cleared north side. Other observers remained outside the fence.

7. The implosion, by which the hulk was leveled, was accompanied by no service, no observance. It was its own statement. Any human words would be superfluous.

By these and other means, counselors and chaplains hoped to ease the pain of people wrenched by catastrophe beyond measure. They wanted to heal as much as possible now to prevent festering in the future. A stitch in time saves nine. When the facial plastic surgeon, Lori Hansen-Lane, was sewing up glass cuts and other injuries, she commented that the quicker you tend a wound, the less scarring will result. It's true emotionally as well as physically.

Tending the New Wound

The service of Healing of Memories, conducted at the Church of the Redeemer in the northwest part of the city, was a unique response to a pressing need. Paramedic Mike McElroy and others saw the need when they experienced firsthand the intense stress this particular catastrophe thrust upon so many. Emergency medical personnel tend to run on adrenaline, keeping extraneous thoughts at bay. They focus on the task and put all else aside. Once the adrenaline surge passes, and the worker gets a rest break, the body idles. Memories crowd in. Doubts assail. Whether deserved or not, guilt sneaks through. The soul cries, "Why?"

There is no such thing as removing memories. They remain. Anything "forgotten" is probably still tucked away somewhere in the brain. Some researchers who specialize in memory point to experiments which demonstrate that every single event in a person's life lives on as a memory. The person who strives to forget may be able to put a memory out of mind; actually, that person is burying it. The conscious no longer sees and hears it, but it hasn't left.

Suppressed, memories fester. Almost invariably, they surface years later, bringing their nastiness back with them. Following the bombing, the ministries of both secular and spiritual counsel therefore sought to prevent memories from being suppressed.

As it was intended, the Healing of Memories service was immensely comforting to many of those who attended, whether they were Christians or not. The devices and elements it used can comfort and help any person who has suffered trauma. Generally, Reverend Robert Wise claims, its success depends not on rote words spoken but on feelings felt. Persons who make themselves available to God will receive God's ministry to the fullest extent.

These techniques are usually used one-on-one with hurting persons. Used in a group setting, they may evoke things that the persons present have sublimated—that is, put out of mind. This can possibly cause more problems than it solves. "Therefore," explains Robert Wise, "we do not often use the service with groups. Sometimes, though, it's justified, as when large numbers of people need similar healing and the wound is fresh. This was one of the times."

The medical personnel at the service varied widely in training, experience, and ability to cope. Each responded uniquely.

So will you. Only you know about your abilities in reference to your personal trauma. Be aware that your response is quite properly yours alone.

The Healing of One EMT Named Sam

Just for purposes of illustration, let's pretend that an EMT—that is, an emergency medical technician—with the fire department retrieved the mutilated corpse of an infant minutes after the bombing. Something like that actually happened, as you know, but we are fictionalizing an event. Our fictionalization reflects upon no one for real.

Let us name our fictional EMT Sam. Sam can be either Samuel or Samantha as you prefer. Female medical personnel were as much a part of the operation as males. The service ministered to both identically.

The Spiritual Basis

The service in which Sam was about to participate was not some ditzy hocus-pocus to make people feel good. It was based upon solid scriptural knowledge of the nature of God. Briefly, the theological basis is this:

Humankind is locked into time but God is not. God functions outside of the constraints of time. Scripture says that Jesus Christ is the same yesterday, today, and forever. Logically, if He can touch people at this moment, He can touch people in the past. Also, Jesus said, "I will never leave you or forsake you."[1] If that is so, Jesus Christ was right there, every moment, at the Alfred P. Murrah building.

The trick then is not to rewrite history but to realize that God in some form (if you wish, borrow the phrase from the twelve-step program, "Higher Power") was present. Taking place in a Christian church under Christian auspices and using a Christian liturgy, the service of healing of memories was based upon the presence of God in the form of Jesus Christ. No surprise there. All were asked to envision Jesus Christ as an agent of God, whether they trusted Him or not, whether they accepted His divinity or not. Any person was invited to take part to whatever extent that person felt comfortable.

The memories, and particularly their emotional aspect, would be brought forward to be touched. Touched by whom was for the participant to decide.

Emotional Connection

You can't deal with a memory while you're trying to suppress it. The technical phrase is, "Getting in emotional touch with the dynamic of the event."

In plain language, it means, "Don't be afraid of your emotional response to the memory, or of your reaction to the event. Let it voice itself."

Sam was trained to keep everyone alive. Retrieving any body is frustrating, but a baby, more so. Sam's emotions therefore would range from horror to sadness to frustration. For Sam, there would be no positive emotion associated with the event.

Some of the medical personnel at the service indeed enjoyed positive emotions. They found survivors and kept them alive. They helped living people escape. They sewed up minor but messy injuries. (Messiness, incidentally, rarely bothers medical people. Most emergency service workers are accustomed to the sight and feel of all manner of body fluids on a trauma site.) Intangible things bother them immensely, however, such as seeing a child mutilated, or detecting incompetence or stupidity in any form whatsoever.

Anger ran rife. Sadness—deep, deep sorrow—pressed heavily on every person there. Sam may have been afraid of the intensity of the anger and sorrow, terrified that it might uncork uncontrolled at the wrong time.

Like so many citizens, Sam might have felt plain, cold fear. That blast occurred at a time no one expected, at a place no one expected, in a way no one expected, destroying innocent lives. You can place yourself in mortal danger by strolling into the Social Security office, by lingering over coffee at the Athenian, by working at your drafting table in Water Resources. Your children enter the supposed safety of day care. No one is safe at any time. That constant at-the-back-of-the-mind fear can enervate.

On top of it all, Sam experienced guilt. Sam felt guilty about not saving people, even the mutilated baby who was impossible to save. Reason never influences guilt; that's why false guilt floats so freely through medical personnel. Sam felt guilty about not doing more. "If only I had gone that second mile." (He or she may already have gone the third. No matter.) Sam felt guilty about feeling guilty, for her reasoning mind was saying, "This is silly" even as her emotional self was screaming "Guilty! Guilty! Guilty!"

These responses and emotions all brought to light where they could not hide and fester; it was time to make connection with the only source of strength that can deal with the heavy, heavy memories.

Spiritual Connection

God was asked to intervene in detectable form as Jesus Christ. Each person there, of course,

172

would experience a different manner and degree of intervention. He was asked to do so thusly:

By means of prayer, God's presence was invoked at that moment. Only God's Spirit can strengthen and truly heal. Only God's wisdom can handle any situation. Sam and the other participants were encouraged to let God take over.

Next, still in prayer, Sam would replay the memory of entering the building, of searching desperately for survivors. Just before the baby was spotted . . .

Wait!

If Jesus promised to stand by His own every moment, He must be there at that moment. The question was not whether God was present; it was, "How can I see Him?"

This, incidentally, is the major question to ask. Our book title—*Where Was God at 9:02 A.M.?*—is not a spiritual question. The biblical question is, "How can I discern Him there?"

The participants were asked to picture Jesus Christ right there in the ruined building where He certainly was, because God had promised so. He simply wasn't visible earlier, as chunks were still falling, as people cried out from somewhere in the debris, as rescuers rushed anxiously from floor to floor. Sam and the others were asked to deliberately see Him as they thought He must be.

At this point, the pastor stepped back out of the picture, so to speak, by no longer making any suggestion as to what to try to see. From now on, the scene would unroll as it would. The pastor was trusting the Spirit of God to guide. For nearly everyone at the service, it did so.

Let's imagine how Sam's new concept of the memory might unfold. Sam might picture Jesus standing beside that baby's physical remains, perhaps even drawing Sam's attention to the tiny form. Jesus was there beside Sam at the retrieval and He followed closely as Sam hurried out of the building. Sam passed the baby to the medical examiner's assistant at the temporary morgue next door, and Jesus watched the transfer, close beside.

A million times, more or less by rote (let's face it), Sam had prayed, "Thy will be done." A million times, Sam had offered to do what God wanted done. Today, in that building, with God's infant in arms, Sam did His will. He needed Sam for a horrible task, and Sam came through for Him.

"It's hard to see anything but God's power and purpose, once you realize He was there," Robert Wise explains.

After the participants rolled the traumatic aspect of their memories to a conclusion, they released all the destructive experiences, the images and pain, into the arms of the risen Christ. Lastly, they were asked to thank Jesus for making Himself known. That was no idle exercise in politeness.

Thankfulness is one of the godliest of traits. It has great power. Too, God desires it.

The service then moved into a bidding prayer of confession and absolution. These are standard in most Christian liturgies, but they served a special purpose here. Through confession and divine absolution, the participant could hold that guilt out for God to see—all the guilt, true and false—and see it dissolved away, forgiven.

Communion, called in some churches the Eucharist or the Lord's Table, followed.

Healing Any Memory

The concept which was employed in this particular service is not limited to severely traumatic memories of the sort generated by the Murrah bombing. It fills other needs as well. Counselors have used it to bring comfort to rape victims, to crime victims, to victims of accidents.

God invites you to call upon Him to help with whatever memories you have which need healing. He wants to hold you as this song, written by one of our contributors, suggests:

We wonder how evil can grip us
As we feel death's lurid detail.
But woven in the wings of destruction
Is a salve, a song that says:

I want to hold you where you are.
I want to hold you where you are.

175

In your desperate, dismal hell
There's nothing left to do
But let me hold you.

I can taste your tears from heaven.
The grief is drenching your soul.
And you my most dearly beloved
Are why I left my home. Oh . . .

You seem so scared of my tenderness.
You run from the sound of my voice.
But I'm with you in your aloneness.
I'm with you, you cannot hide.

I want to hold you where you are.
I want to hold you where you are.
I know your momma, your baby,
your sister is gone.
I want to hold you where you are.
Please let me hold you.[2]

Giving Thanks

We drum it into our two-year-olds. Say thank you, child, so as to appear polite and well brought up.

No, no, no. It goes infinitely deeper than that. Giving thanks is no small gesture. Over and over, God tells His people that He expects thanks. Some time, look up *thanks* and *thanksgiving* in a concordance and read the passages. Giving thanks is a very big deal to God, and it is therefore immensely satisfying to humankind, who reflect His image.

Over and over, recovering survivors say, "I want to find out who my rescuers were and thank them."

The state of Oklahoma corporately gave thanks. We put full-page, full-color ads in *USA Today, Newsweek, U.S. News and World Report,* and *Time.* The newspapers and magazines donated the space, saving Oklahoma $452,000. That money will go into the relief effort. The state will put the thank-you on posters to send to the out-of-state workers who came to help, the cost being raised in the private sector so that it won't come out of taxpayers' pockets.

And our Fourth of July celebration recognized the many search and rescue units who helped us.

That gesture of thanks is not a frill. It is a strong impetus to healing.

Moving On

Healing does not happen instantly. People who participated in the service, in the debriefing, in prayer, had a big head start on dealing with traumatic memories. But there was much more to be done.

CHAPTER TEN

Stepping Past Loss—Healing the Pain

RATHER LIKE BABE RUTH, WHO POINTED out where his home run was going to go, the demolition expert who was about to fell the Murrah hulk pointed to the curb on the north side of 5th. The building's rubble, he declared, would spread no farther than here. The walls would collapse inward, the elevator tower would fall northward, and it would all sort of fold onto itself.

The demolisher was orchestrating a healing act.

Early Tuesday morning, May 23, over two thousand people gathered in the area around the hulk of the Murrah building to watch what was left of it go down. Some carried flowers. The EMS personnel who served during the tragedy were grouped with the president of their association beside a barrier tape. Survivors and people whose loved ones died clustered together, trusting each other to help cushion the loss. Firefighters watched with firefighters.

At 7:01 A.M., a little puff of smoke erupted near the base of the hulk. Less than eight seconds later, the building lay flat on the ground somewhere inside a rising, ten-story dust cloud. Most of the watchers hardly had time to gasp.

Priscilla Salyers reached for her fifteen-year-old son who was behind her. Instead, a woman she'd never met before, Elsie Stibral, reached out to her, totally overcome. They hugged. Other people gaped. They sobbed. They wept openly. Some simply nodded, totally composed.

The building's cylindrical corner columns lay like the ruins of Ozymandias—the fallen colossus in Percy Bysshe Shelley's poem—laced with breaks and cracks but still carrying echoes of their original strength. And in the middle, where the first-floor Social Security office once served thousands, a massive mound of debris covered all. The demolition crew had put the whole thing exactly where they said they would. Gray dust powdered the street and sidewalks, but you could still clearly see the curb marking the north side of 5th. The building's rubble had spread that far and no farther.

As the dust dispersed, so did the crowd.

It was over.

It was beginning.

Short-Term Steps to Healing

For many people that May 23, the collapse of the Alfred P. Murrah hulk marked closure. Some comments:

- "Now the healing can start."
- "Now maybe we can begin to put this behind us."
- "We didn't want that sitting there as a symbol of destruction." [referring to the remains of the building]

Find a Means of Closure

Closure is exactly what the word sounds like. Close the book. Close the lid. Close the door. It does not mean forgetting. It does not even mean forgiving. It is merely a line drawn. And it is necessary to the healing process.

A traumatic memory or loss should have some definite point which the owner of that loss or memory can identify as the end or the beginning of the end of the traumatic event. These points of closure vary infinitely, even as people vary. No two will be the same. When many people share one experience, as occurred when the Murrah hulk was collapsed, their perceptions of it will vary individually.

An Event as Closure

For example, to Edye Smith, who lost two small sons, "It's not really closing or opening a chapter.

181

It's not that emotional for me." She had closed her chapter in other ways. Still, the demolition hit her hard in other ways. At the moment the building imploded, she murmured, stunned, "Oh, my God."[1]

Another said, "It's time Oklahoma began to put this behind." She then added, "I'd like to see the flags back at full staff again." For that person, probably, the flags more so than the implosion would close the door. They did so for many. Oklahoma brought the flags, at half mast since April 19, back to full mast on the Fourth of July at 9:02 A.M., as a drum rolled and four F-16 fighter planes roared overhead.

Said Governor Keating of the U.S. flag, "It flew from the damaged building, it shone proudly from the uniforms of the rescue workers, and it draped the caskets of the victims. It was stained and it was torn, but it was beautiful."

Ron Norick, the mayor of Oklahoma City, said: "I think today is the best day . . . to have the governor raise the flags so we can get back to the lives we love so well."

That's closure.

Closure may come with something as simple as returning to look at the scene. Says an observer, "I visited the site in late June. It was maybe 95 degrees. A scattering of people still came and went, peering through the fence. Flowers, ribbons, and other mementos adorned it.

"Some people would stand at the fence, and you could see from the expressions on their faces that they were looking light years beyond the site. Whatever the processes going on inside them, it was, we can hope, a healing experience.

"Others were obviously gawkers being escorted by locals. A car would drive by without stopping; sometimes without even slowing down at all. The window would roll down, an arm would stick itself out and point to the site, it would pull back in, and then the window would roll up. Don't want the air conditioner to have to work over-time. End of emotional experience."

Ritual as Closure

Usually closure involves a ritual. Funerals serve exactly that purpose. They are universally recognized as a formal good-bye said by the living to the dead. In our culture they are not conducted for the benefit of the dead. As a classical radio station disc jockey once commented, "Haydn asked that they perform that [last work played] at his funeral. We don't know whether they did. Neither did Haydn."

Some people consider ritual to be hollow. Hardly so. Ritual is a convenience, ideally a familiar form that takes no one by surprise, enabling all to partake to whatever extent they care to. Some people turn off portions of a funeral that don't interest them; others dwell upon every detail.

Usually, the funeral comes at a time when the bereaved are numb anyway. The established pattern helps them do what they want done without having to think too much about it.

When Reverend Robert Wise conducted the Healing of Memories service, he placed it in the context of church ritual. Certainly it was reaching out to God. But you don't need a church ritual to address Him. The ritual made human beings comfortable so that all could participate at whatever level they cared to.

"A good service," claims Robert Wise, "is a prism redirecting the Light. It spreads the focused love of God into a wide spectrum of results achieved."

Some religious groups practice anointing. Others hold wakes. Valerie Koelsch's wake drew seven hundred, her funeral one thousand. It was the kind of enthusiastic good-bye that put a lovely exclamation point to her exuberant life.

An Act as Closure

A Reunion with Rescuers At 9:02 Randy Ledger's carotid artery was severed and he was losing blood by the quart. In a short time, he would lose two-thirds of his blood. He didn't know that until some time later. He didn't know the people who saved his life, either—a police officer, an emergency medical attendant, an intern, and a restaurateur. In the hospital, he learned that the police officer and the restaurateur carried him out of the Murrah building, and during that evacuation the officer broke through the rubble and hurt his back. In fact, the officer and Randy rode to the hospital together in the same ambulance.

Completely disabled in his hospital bed, Randy could not communicate for days. He would recover well, although his prospects didn't look too bright for a while. People die when drained of two-thirds of their blood, but miraculously, Randy lived. The miracles didn't end there, however.

Monday morning, Randy's family were trying to find the names of the people to whom Randy owed his life. All his sister knew was that a police officer hurt his back during the rescue, so she called Presbyterian Hospital. A few minutes later, that very person, Terry Yeakey, called the hospital asking about a patient he had helped Wednesday. He thought the man was named Randy. Both calls were channeled to the same person.

"It's like God was directing us together," Yeakey commented.

Weeks later, nearly recovered, Randy Ledger sat down to dinner in a restaurant with a few good men. Terry Yeakey, Peter Schaffer, the restaurateur from the Grateful Bean who helped carry him out, EMT Daryl Wood who kept him alive on the ride to the hospital, and Dr. Paul Preslar, who "corked the hole" in his carotid.

Finding those men and buying them dinner was the act of closure Randy Ledger needed to complete that episode of his life. It satisfied. It was the sigh at the end of a story. And the act of closure was just as important to the others, Yeakey in particular. Need we mention, Randy picked up the check?

A reunion with rescuers brought closure for Randy. Another type of reunion brought the same closure for Fred Kubasta and Ernie Ross.

A Reunion of Survivors   Fred Kubasta and Ernie Ross worked down in the composing room of the *Journal-Record,* the newspaper housed across from the Murrah building. Both were severely lacerated in the blast; neither knew how he himself got out or whether his buddy had made it at all. When Bud Tatum, a Red Cross worker, got to the site minutes after the blast, he helped Ernie to the triage center and worked diligently to get the man's bleeding under control. Ernie happened to glance at the form next to him. It was Fred.

Despite Bud's request to lie still, Ernie reached out and brushed his friend with his fingertips, the only contact he could manage. "Fred, I'm here."

That simple gesture touched Bud Tatum deeply. In horror and extremity, one person cared enough for another to reach out. He yearned to find the two men whose names he wasn't even sure he knew. Fred was one, apparently. Did his patient mention that his own name was Ernie? He thought so. They were both in bad shape. Did they survive beyond his care?

Bud and his wife were interviewed in the *Daily Oklahoman.* The interview ended with Bud's quote,

"It has been a tremendous thing to see this community and the whole state and nation respond to this disaster. They really did it, and this is what love is all about—but I really would like to know who Fred and Ernie are—I would really like to know."

About a month later, the three were reunited. Said Bud, "I never wanted to put my arms around two men so much in my life."

Closure, you see. An episode completed, the ends tucked in.

An Act, a Ritual, and an Event Pamela Briggs combined them all—an act, a ritual, an event—when she received her Bachelor of Arts in Business Administration at University of Oklahoma graduation exercises on May 13. Her fierce determination to attend the ceremonies—"If they won't release me, I'll try to get a pass for the day"—was the first clue that this would act as closure. As she sat in her wheelchair beside the rest of the graduating class with her tasseled mortarboard square upon her head, university president David Boren brought her diploma to her. The standing ovation by the fifteen thousand attendees there overwhelmed her.[2]

She had been released from the hospital that morning. She experienced closure.

Unfortunately sometimes closure is thwarted.

Closure Thwarted When the search ended with two and probably three bodies still buried in the rubble, Oklahoma City's firefighters had a hard time backing off. From the beginning it was they alone who handled remains. They said of the victims, "These are our own." They didn't want to quit short of completing the job.

After the implosion, workers moved in and recommenced digging as the city firefighters waited. One evening, the supervisor guessed, "Probably tomorrow." The firefighters went home. A short time later, the workers came upon the bodies and removed them.

Ever gracious, the firefighters allowed that the important thing was that all the missing were now retrieved, but their disappointment was palpable. That disappointment was not at all selfishness or ego. It was closure thwarted.

It is unfortunate, and very sad, that the supervisor did not realize the importance of closure, not just for the individuals of the fire department but for the department as a corporate entity as well. They needed a sense of completion that will always be just a little bit lacking.

Closure is not only for the person affected. It bears an impact on others just as much. When Trudy Rigney received her earned degree posthumously from the University of Oklahoma, the act was primarily for others. As Pam Briggs received the ovation and her diploma, the brother of Michael Thompson, one of the lost, sat nearby (he's an official of the university). His wound was far too deep and ragged to find closure in this place.

If you have recently experienced trauma or loss, is there something you yearn to do? . . . Really hunger to do? Bud Tatum wanted badly to find those two men. The firefighters wanted badly to bring out the last victims. What do you want really badly? For you, that might be the act of closure that will put the period at the end of your sentence.

If it is something impossible, such as, "I want to bring back that horrible moment and relive it another way," you'll have to adjust your desire into something possible. Not everyone has an imploding building upon which to hang closure, but perhaps you can think of something similar. Visiting a place, doing a particular thing, performing a ritual of your choice, meeting a person or persons—consider, and then do.

Some of the best acts of closure involve doing something. Also, doing something is itself a healing tool. It usually works best if the action is performed soon after the loss.

Do Something

Do Something Ordinary

Harve Speakes parked his United Parcel Service truck by the Murrah building, scooped up his two deliver-before-10:30 packages, hopped to the curb, and jogged inside. He delivered one to the administrative office, for which Pam Briggs signed, and took the elevator to the fifth floor. George Decker in VA signed for the other and Harve headed back down to his truck. It was 8:57 A.M.

He drove east to Broadway, turned north, and stopped for another delivery. The blast lifted his truck off its wheels and tossed all his shelved parcels into a heap. The first rumors to circulate suggested a package bomb and for several hours, until the reality became known, he wondered if perhaps he had delivered it.

Pam Briggs and George Decker both survived. Many of Harve's "signature buddies"—people who signed for deliveries—did not. A big chunk of his route is gone. Had he been two or three minutes slower that morning, he would have vaporized. Traumatic loss is going to be camping on Harve's doorstep for some time to come.

Said Harve, "I pray for a workload to keep me busy."[3]

Harve was onto an excellent healing device— normalcy. Taking refuge in routine.

Many survivors say that they found comfort in routine. Routine is so normal, a welcome counterpoint to the hideously abnormal events you just suffered. Survivor Lorri McNiven noted, however, that at first, as she began picking up the pieces of her life, regular chores took twice as long to complete. It wasn't easy, gearing back up to normal. [4]

She made another important observation, para-phrased: Only when the survivors get back to work will healing really begin; the missing co-workers will affect survivors even more than the funerals. True. Funerals are closure, and closure is only one aspect of healing.

"It was so hard to go back [to work]," claimed several survivors, echoing a common thought. Yes. Missing coworkers or no, the person return-ing to routine usually must force the return. You really don't want to. It really does help.

Melissa McCulley, who at 9:02 was buried in debris on the first floor, went back to work, but it was not routine. "Everything's hectic because we lost everything and we lost people in the office. . . . It's going to take awhile before we get back to normal." Still, she is doing her part to bring things back to normal, and that in itself is healing. Activity out of the ordinary can help also.[5]

Do Something Out of the Ordinary

At St. John's Episcopal School, four children lost their grandparents in the blast, and the relatives of two of St. John's preschoolers were injured. It hap-pened, too, that in a corner of the schoolyard stood two walls, the ruins of a farmhouse on the property. The roof, long gone, had been replaced by arching hackberry trees. It was a lovely spot, bathed in gentle neglect.

The school's headmistress, Sherry Rowan, spear-headed a movement to turn the corner into an open-air chapel dedicated to victims of violence—not just the beloved grandparents, but others as well. The kids held fund-raisers to buy stone benches. They painted messages on tiles, and House of Clay, a local company, glazed them free of charge. Dona-tions and that endless resource, parent labor, turned the corner into a beautiful monument to victory over death.[6]

Although only a few children suffered direct loss, all were affected, many of them deeply. With the chapel project, they all had something they could do. So, for that matter, did the parents and donors. Human beings are created to be partici-pants. Doing something is incredibly healing.

What can you do? Ideally, the action you con-sider will hinge in some way upon the loss or trauma you suffered. Let's use a fictional "for instance."

Let's say you lost a dear friend in the Murrah bombing, but you live in Decatur, Illinois. Your friend loved the zoo in Oklahoma City, and talked about it in letters and phone calls. You might set up a volunteer gig at the zoo in the memory of your friend and take a week's vacation to go down and perform the service. You feel better; your friend's memory is honored; the zoo she loved benefits.

But maybe that's not possible, or your friend had no special interest you can serve. There's nothing you can do in Oklahoma. You might dedicate an unrelated activity to the memory of your friend, any activity, including a local one. Perhaps you like the Adopt-a-Highway Program through which local groups can keep highway litter at bay. Sign up. Picking up litter along a section of highway in the memory of a lost loved one is doing something meaningful, even though the loved one may never have driven that section of the highway.

Do not discount donating money as well as effort—money represents effort, once removed—but don't limit your thinking to monetary donation. Physical participation is very satisfying. So is service.

Perform Service to Others

It just so happens (secular analysts ascribed it to fate; those who believe in God know better) that the local Norman (Oklahoma) chapter of Compassionate Friends met about twelve hours before the bomb exploded. The Oklahoma City chapter had met less than a week before. There are twelve such chapters just in Oklahoma.

Compassionate Friends, established in 1980, is a mutual-support group of parents who have lost children. Their calling later expanded to embrace children who lost parents. Before the dust cleared, they were making contact with funeral homes and churches, giving them information on how bereaved parents can make arrangements. Newspapers picked them up and published phone numbers. The comfort offered by Compassionate Friends extends for years beyond the event mourned—as long as it takes. Comforted members then pass the comfort on.

Compassionate Friends serves both the recipients of their service and the servers themselves. All such service groups do. It's a win-win situation. People whose loss is raw need help. As their reaction to their loss matures, they also need *to* help. Helping others is immensely healing, for it not only directs interest away from the hurting self, it provides something to do.

Let's set up another fictional situation. Your friend, an older gentleman who has just suffered loss, fumes, "I don't like that touchy-feely stuff. Support groups? Bah! A waste of time."

Don't push it. Service to others helps healing. It does not have to take a particular form. If support groups (or your personal favorite service organization) fail to appeal to him, how about Lions Club International? They pursue worthy service projects and provide excellent camaraderie. Kiwanis? March of Dimes? Red Cross? Humane Society? The local garden club who cleans up the park every spring and fall? What can you suggest to your friend that will appeal to his interests, serve others, and serve him?

The companionship these organizations offer is as important to the person who is healing as is the actual service.

Find People to Be With

The natural tendency of the person who suffers loss is to separate. To isolate. This generation as a whole does not remember Greta Garbo's famous movie line which defined a whole mind-set: "I vahnt to be alone."

Come to think of it, this generation probably doesn't remember Greta Garbo. She was famous not just for her movie work but for her off-camera aura of mystery and reclusiveness. Glamour personified.

Join Together with Others

There is nothing glamorous about debilitating trauma and loss. The first line of defense against too much introspection and self-pity is family. So many survivors echo, "Family and friends are so much more important now." They are important to the healing process also, and easy to wall away.

Rick Edington, who took the blast from his office in the Journal-Record building across the street, told an interviewer, "Certainly it's affected my life! I've reassessed my priorities, and I've easily seen that people are a lot more caring than I had ever imagined."[7]

Reassessed priorities. For the survivor of loss and trauma, that's not nearly as easy as it sounds. The natural tendency to tunnel into oneself must be overcome.

The survivor ought also look to people beyond family and close friends. If need be, pick a group that reflects an interest or something you might like to try. How about the local woodcarving club (yes, there is one)? Astronomy group? Ask at the library about bird-watchers in the area or old movie buffs. You'd be amazed. The bottom line, the ultimate trick, is to get out beyond yourself into another world, another interest.

Pray for Others

Praying for others is expected of believers in many faiths. The act of prayer is healing in that it turns our focus outward. And of course, that's not to mention that prayer is the will of God.

A German man living in England during the 1800s, George Mueller, started four orphanages through the power of prayer. His story is fascinating. As part of that feat, he kept a log of prayer. He wrote requests in one column and dated them. He wrote the answers in the other column and dated them. Very, very often, the dates were identical.

We suggest you make your own prayer log—people prayed for and, if you wish, results that you are able to discern.

Tell Your Story to Others

Tell it to friends. Tell it to a newspaper. Draw pictures of it. Write poems about it. Hundreds and hundreds of poems were written in the weeks following the bombing. They vary widely in quality, of course, but they come from the heart, and it is the heart that must heal. Never discount the arts—drama, writing, poetry, drawing—as healing aids.

There are many other devices, but they are more of a long-range nature. Let's look at them next.

Long-Range Strategies

The Grieving Process

Most people for one reason or another cannot wait for the long-range healing process to make its effects felt. Children facing school, people who must earn a living, and many others must work past the worst of the trauma quickly and get back to a fairly competent level of function. That's where the short-range techniques we've just explored can help. They stop the gaps until the healing balm of grief completes its work.

The grieving process might advance smoothly, or it can take a painfully long time. The amount of time it takes has nothing to do with the griever's skills or abilities. It does not correlate directly with the size of the loss. "It should not be taking this long" is nearly always a false statement. The by-stander's "You can't be through it that fast" is also.

Everybody, probably, has heard about the steps in the grieving process. You need not be a psychologist or counselor to know and practice them. We won't go into them in detail, but we felt that a book of this nature really ought to have them, just as reference. In order to provide you with the steps, we are including them as Appendix E.

The Physiological Aspect

One of the major reasons that grief takes time is that it possesses a strong physiological component. That is, your body chemistry changes. Specifically, this is what happens.

None of the cell tips in that convoluted mass that is your brain actually touch each other. The cells, called neurons, have many threads (called axons), like spider legs, whose tips come close to the tips of all the other cells' threads. Messages are conveyed by extremely small electrical pulses.

To complete a thought or thought connection, a neuron produces a tiny, tiny droplet of chemical called a neurotransmitter right out at the appropriate tip. That chemical connects the tip with another so that the electrical pulse can flow from cell to cell.

When a person is sad and grieving, the cells produce less of that chemical and keep less of it available. Cheer flees. Life slows down. Eventually, chemical production picks back up and the person recovers that old sparkle. If for some reason the production of neurotransmitters remains inadequate, depression results. Should depression persist too long, the brain may completely lose its ability to restore full production and use of neurotransmitters. We call that *dysthymia*—chronic or low-grade depression. Then, chemical production may be augmented with a drug until the brain can get back to producing the necessary neurotransmitters on its own.

It is important to understand that this physiological aspect has a big say in recovery and sticks to its own time schedule, so you cannot expect a quick snapback on some other, arbitrary schedule. You can't rush Mother Nature.

Until Grieving Abates

As a public health service, the *Daily Oklahoman* has been publishing information and help for people dealing with post-traumatic stress and loss. The paper provides a number of Access Line extensions for anything from songs you might listen to, to means for spilling your guts (listed by its extension number as "Express your feelings").

Fortunately, the state as an entity recognizes that many people will need help dealing in positive ways with grief. Her citizens have not been hung out to dry on their own.

199

Beyond Grief

What can those in Oklahoma City do? What can anyone do? Let grief run its course. Eventually, we all come to grips with the fact that pain is inevitable.

But suffering is optional.

Somehow, that verity runs against the grain of our society in the United States. The prevailing message is that being a victim pays. The more you suffer, the more you reap. Or try to.

Not so. It is in fact a part of the healing process to take the suffering and raise it to a new level of awareness of God and man and life itself.

The grieving process mends the hurt. That is not the ultimate goal. Wisdom is. In the fullness of time, suffering can produce either answers to questions or a measure of contentment with the lack of answers.

Very, very frequently the answers come, bringing a measure of peace, but the person who has worked out those answers cannot articulate them to others. "I understand, but I can't explain it." Many people can honestly say that, and no wonder. Some things are deeper and more complex than mere words can frame. To quote the old adage, "The flowering thoughts of our minds lose half their petals in our speech."

Suffering does not automatically produce illumination, however. It can remain suffering for a lifetime. Pain but no peace. Complete healing comes, if it comes, long beyond the actual grief. The search for ultimate truth does not always come to fruit. But only ignorance refuses to seek. Only ignorance relaxes in pat answers. Ignorance never furthers healing.

Let's look for some of the answers to the difficult questions raised by the Murrah bombing next.

CHAPTER ELEVEN

Where Was God at 9:01 A.M.?

THE WEEKS AFTER APRIL 19, 1995 WERE a time for questioning and introspection. More than one radio or television reporter or commentator prowled the streets of Oklahoma City asking interviewees, "Are you mad at God?"

Mike McElroy, a paramedic, smiles at the thought: "I was downtown a few minutes after it happened; it's where I usually work.

"It's interesting. If someone posed that question on the street, someone else would jump in with, 'Listen! This was not of God! This was pure evil.' It didn't matter if the person answering was the person being asked or not.

"And the response of the community and the children. We in the medical services have gotten maybe three hundred, four hundred cards and letters. That's just us. Rescuers are getting truckloads too. Ninety percent of them mention God. Spontaneous letters. Kids from ages four to teenage. Most of them not from Christian schools. These are so-called secular kids.

"They say, 'God bless you'; 'Don't worry, God is with you'; 'Don't worry, God is there.'

"Georgia, Michigan, all over. They tell us they're praying for us, God is with us, press on."

Mike continues, obviously waxing eloquent on a favorite subject. "It's fascinating. The hand of evil was recognized immediately, and I don't mean by theologians. These are the people I talked to all the time downtown, what you'd call the everyday people. Almost a hundred percent agreement; this was not of God, but how can we use it to God's purpose?

"Perfect strangers would stop me—we'd be out in the ambulance on call and we'd roll down the window and talk—and these people would want to talk about the bombing, and about their relationship to God. It's uncanny how often that happened. And they'd start out on the relationship part with, 'It's been a long time. . . .'

"I can understand. One look at that building, and the fragility of life comes home very hard."

His eyes mist. "God bless the small children."

The Deeper Questions

Let us offer some questions and observations that people in Oklahoma grapple with now. They are not new. People have been grappling with them since time began. We have the written record of that exploration dating from, probably, around 1500 B.C., the conservative dating of the book of Job in the Hebrew Scripture. They take on a fresh urgency as the wounds from Oklahoma City scab over.

Where was God at 9:02 A.M.? We answered that. Oklahoma City, the same as He was at Calvary Hill while His Son died. Evidence of His presence was everywhere.

People ask, though, an even more pressing question: "Where was God at 9:01 A.M.?" There's the rub. If He was there, why did He allow babies to die so horribly, not to mention the others? And there are several hard choices.

Did He instigate it?

Did He passively allow it?

Did He lack the power to prevent it?

Free Choice

Most people wrestling with that question—in conversation, in sermons, in essays and columns—point first to the free will which God gave humankind. The basis of it, briefly, is this: Loving God if you have no choice but to love God is not loving Him. The same goes for obeying Him. If

205

you have no choice, that's not obedience. For several reasons, which would take a whole book to explore, God gave humankind free choice, so that our love and our obedience would be real.

The flip side, of course, is that we can choose wrong if we wish.

The Nature of Evil

Satan, according to both Jewish and Christian theology, once served God with a rank at least equal to that of the archangel Michael. Not content with that station, he defied God and tried to place himself on a par with the Almighty. About a third of the created angels sided with him in a cosmic power play beyond ken. Incidentally, if this is true, think what a brilliant manipulator he must is to convince so many intelligent servants of God that he was powerful enough to oppose the Shaddai and win! God cast him and those with him out of His presence, and the rest, as they say, is history.

This is the basis from which many theologians declare that evil is the absence of contact with God. God is the ultimate good, which makes Satan the ultimate evil, though never at the same level as God (His level, remember, is that of Michael). Satan is spirit, but he is not divine.

One of Satan's names, Lucifer, comes from the Latin *lux,* lucis, meaning *light.* Once upon a time, Satan was light. The light was extinguished by his rebellion. Jesus warned us, "Satan transforms himself into an angel of light."[1] And angel he is; of light he is not.

The situation extends to humankind. The farther a person is separated from God, the more that person is vulnerable to evil thoughts and deeds. Ultimate separation, ultimate evil. That's the theological theory.

Still fighting God, Satan may or may not realize he can't win. Certainly, he is going to ally whomever he can to his side, manipulating humankind to his purposes as much as possible.

A secular example is Ann Rice's series of novels about vampires. The vampire Lestat demonstrates an icy skill in manipulating the vulnerable and the unwitting into serving Lestat's perverted appetites. It's a splendid picture of Satan if you keep in mind that he's even more evil than that.

Bishop Fulton J. Sheen was fond of saying, "The devil wants us to think he doesn't exist, so he is always circulating the news of his death."

Many theologians would nod agreement with the bishop and add, "But don't you believe it."

So let's say that the person who perpetrated the bomb, whoever that person might be, claims he or she did it because God said to. Or that the perpetrator claims to be a Christian, devoted to the will and furtherance of Jesus Christ. This is not in the least out of the question.

Is that person actually allied to God? The theologian would say, "Totally separated from God. Totally misled by Lucifer. Allied to Satan and thinking this was of God."

The question becomes, then, who's got the juice, God or Satan? How much power does each of these opposing forces really possess? How far can one control the other?

Power Balance

Near Guy, Arkansas, in the foothills of the Ozarks, horse and cattle operations spread their fences across the rolling green pastureland. In that bucolic landscape, one set of fencing, enclosing several acres, looks pretty much the same as all the rest, until you get up close. Then you notice that the fence is made out of welded railroad rails and the posts are eight feet tall. You learn that those great steel posts are sunk seven feet into the ground. It's Scott Riddle's farm.

Scott raises elephants.

Powerful as Scott's animals are, they can only go so far, to the fence and no farther. They can kill a human being and many elephants (though none of Scott's) have done so. They can ride a mature tree down and break it off. They can wreak havoc, given the opportunity. They can do a lot of things. But at Scott's farm, they can only go so far.

Some theologians believe that is something like the power balance between God and Satan here on Earth. Satan misleads godless men, but God allows him to go only so far. Satan can perpetrate much evil, but only so far. Only if God withdraws, allowing Satan's boundaries to expand, might Satan go farther—move the fence out, as it were. And Scripture suggests that that indeed might happen as the end of history as we know it draws near.

This theological concept, that Satan is limited by certain parameters, comes from, among other places, the first chapter of the Hebrew book of Job.

Job is a good man who loves God, Satan claims, because God has blessed him so. Take away these blessings, Job says, and he'll turn from you.

God disagrees. He allows Satan to test Job: The devil may take away his wealth, but may not take his life.

Some may ask, "Why let Satan operate at all?" Free choice. But God doesn't let it rest there. Instead He used the cosmic power balance between Him and Satan to pull the most magnificent coup this world will ever see.

It happened one day almost two thousand years ago on a hill called Golgotha. Here, Satan thinks he's going to commit the ultimate sacrilege by killing the one person on earth least deserving of death, not to mention that it's God's own Son. As we know, Satan gets away with it. There hangs his nemesis, Jesus Christ, in agony on a cross, wailing, "My God, why have You forsaken Me?"[2] Victory over God Himself! Yes!

Does Satan celebrate? If so, it's premature. Three days later, Satan watches Jesus walk out of His tomb. Worst of all from Satan's viewpoint, God declares that undeserving death to be adequate payment for any and all human wrongdoing. Satan's whole master plan for humankind has just been pitched into the dumpster.

What a magnificent turning of the tables! God switched the ultimate act of evil, murdering His innocent Son, into the ultimate act of mercy and love! You know the verse; you've heard it often: "For God so loved the world that He gave His only begotten Son, that whoever believes in Him should not perish but have everlasting life."[3] It's God's victory of love over the darkest machinations of evil.

To what extent God allowed evil in Oklahoma, we will never really know. Where Satan's boundaries are, we will never really know. Much too close; that's for sure. All of this is what Billy Graham in his address at the memorial service that Sunday following the blast, referred to as a mystery.

So does Reverend Robert Wise. "What remains after my deepest inquiry is exhausted is mystery."

Or another pastor, with a grin and a helpless shrug, "Don't ask me. I'm in sales, not management."

No matter how much you try to pick this apart and figure it out, God's infinite wisdom still extends too far beyond us to see.

In Oklahoma

The Alfred P. Murrah building at 9:02 A.M. was not the ultimate act of evil. But to those of us who lived through the bombing, it seems so. It seems so. Healing will take years. We do know that God is involved. He was here, He is still here, and He can bless us through this. Most importantly, He will be glorified.

We feel just like Job, beleaguered and hurting. We as a state can identify with that whole first two chapters of the book of Job, and take immense comfort in them. Satan expected Job to buckle under adversity and Job did not. He came out of it stronger. So shall we. Despite a lot of bad advice, as the text says, "In all this Job did not sin nor charge God with wrong."[4]

And in pride and love, God boasts, "Consider My servant Oklahoma. . . ." [5]

One Survivor's Answer to the Question "Where Was God?"

Randy Ledger, the survivor who made closure by taking his rescuers to dinner, wrote out his own answer to the question "Where was God?" six weeks after the blast. In part:

211

"He was with me when my friend Mike Louden-slager discovered my almost lifeless body and, when he went to get help, lost his own life. . . ."

He then lists those who helped and tended him, identifying nineteen by name and alluding to many others.

He continues: "Finally, He was with the loving and caring multitudes who gave so much of themselves by volunteering, giving, writing, and cheerfully working. He has always been there. He will always be there. He will never leave me nor forsake me."

The bombing was not an act of God. It was an act of man, of madness. Do not confuse the two. God will use human choices—good or bad—for His own plans and His own glory. From a horrible tragedy has come wondrous love and compassion.

We could not have said it better.

CHAPTER TWELVE

Why Did Some Live and Others Die?

FIREFIGHTERS WERE SWARMING ALL over the building during the first few hours after the bombing. They were poking around down in the basement and plowing through the debris on the gaping floors. Every now and then, the footing would sag or shimmy, reminding everyone that the whole thing could go at any time. Desks, they soon learned, were under those mounds of ceiling tiles, light fixtures, sprinkler pipes, and unidentifiable rubble, so they concentrated on the mounds.

At this point, they were still ignoring the dead in order to scramble and find the living.

Bobby Lax, a firefighter and paramedic who drove an ambulance as well, was working beside ten other firefighters, clawing through wreckage on the fourth floor when word came up from the basement: "We have a live one!"

People down there heard tapping. They knew it wasn't just the random clicks and ticks as the tortured rubble settled. This tapping was putting out an SOS in Morse code!

Being a paramedic, Bobby hurried down the stairs to help out. Minutes later, he found himself crawling around in the black, unlighted, debris-choked basement with two other guys, the rest of the rescuers somewhere behind them.

"Be quiet! I think I heard something."

They had to work their way past a corpse so badly mangled that they wouldn't have been able to determine the person's gender but for some rings on the cooling fingers. That was work for later. They had a live one.

Bobby crawled across shifting debris. So far he hadn't thought much about what they were doing, or what they had to pass to reach that tapping. Then, stretching as far as he could, he touched her hand. Her living hand.

"The most intense emotion hit me." Suddenly it rushed on him—really hit him—what they were doing there and why. It was no longer a pro-tracted disaster drill. This was life and death; he had just passed death to serve life. All sorts of heavy meanings crashed upon him. It was no longer a heady, adrenaline-powered dash.

They had a live one!

Bobby and the others managed to move enough broken wreckage that the woman could twist around and change her body configuration so that they could pull her out. They fitted a protective cervical collar around her neck just in case there was some spinal injury, and strapped her securely to a backboard.

She said her name was Sheara Gamble.

At about this point, Bobby realized that he and his buddies hadn't been thinking very far ahead. Working their way in here to reach her had taken them an inordinately long time. Now they were going to have to crawl back out over this jumbled pile of loose wreckage hauling a loaded backboard, and keep their packaged patient safe in the bargain. No way. Not in this lifetime.

He twisted around to scan the pile and maybe pick out a shorter or easier route. He stared. Before them stretched an open superhighway. While he and his buddies were concentrating on digging their patient free and preparing her in order to prevent any further chance of injury, the people behind him had cleared the floor all the way to the east door!

It Shall Be a Sign

In a wrecked basement heaped with debris, the only sound the drip of blood, the only light a few thin beams from flashlights, Morse code. SOS. Sheara Gamble lived. Yet Charles Hurlburt, a great-grandson of Samuel Morse, who invented this code, and his wife, Jean, died in the Murrah building at 9:02 A.M. Why did Sheara live and Charles and his wife die?

Eighteen children died that day. But others were spared. At the Civic Center downtown, the Oklahoma City Philharmonic Orchestra was preparing for a children's concert. From all over the state, three thousand schoolkids were being bussed in. Ed Walker, the orchestra's manager, had even picked up his walkie-talkie to start coordinating the arrival of about one hundred buses. What with downtown's one-way streets, the drivers were going to have to circle around through a few blocks to reach the Civic Center. Had the bomb gone off half an hour later, some of those laden school buses would have been passing the Murrah building.

And then there is the story of two parents who were searching for any sign of their children that day. Frantic with worry, Jim Denny and his wife Claudia had found each other at the bomb site. Now they waited helplessly at the Red Cross center. Their two children, ages two and three, had been in the America's Kids day-care center in the Murrah building.

As they watched TV coverage of the scene, a television news reporter announced that an unidentified little girl with red hair had been taken to Southwest Medical Center where she was undergoing surgery.

"There's only one of those!" Jim and Claudia hurried down to Southwestern for a reunion with their daughter Rebecca.

"God had given me one miracle," said Jim. "Why not throw two my way?"

He did.

The Dennys heard about a boy at Presbyterian, a strawberry blond. They headed north uptown to their three-year-old Brandon.

A Red Cross worker who watched the Dennys leave on the way to their Rebecca purred, "And they say television is a vast wasteland." [1]

The Dennys experienced a miracle. Their children were alive. Yet eighteen others died that day.

The question, "Why did some live and others die?" reverberates throughout the stories from Oklahoma City. Thousands, literally thousands, of people relate stories that resemble Sheara Gamble and the Dennys. People who were miraculously saved. Or persons who set up some alternative to the routine which altered their course and quite possibly saved their lives, like Liz Thomas. We might call them "near-miss" stories.

Liz Thomas and three friends in Social Security were sent to the stockroom at 8:30 A.M. on Wednesday morning with the job of reorganizing old files in the stockroom. Go through the records, throw out some stuff, file the rest.

"I said, 'I really ought to go open the customer reception window. It's nine, and we have a room full of claimants out there.'

"But my friend said, 'Let's go through this one stack.' Suddenly the metal shelves were flying. They fell above us like an A frame and protected us—one of those near misses. Much later—not at that time—we would realize that the noise we heard just then was the concrete floors collapsing. And we could hear the glass. It went dark and very quiet. Water sprayed down on us and we were afraid we might drown. We started yelling for help."

The assistant manager called down to them from above, answering them. They used that steel shelf as a ladder to climb out onto rubble eight to ten feet deep. Objects were falling down on them from above. A chunk of Sheetrock dropped on Liz's head; a computer fell in front of her—but fell face down so the glass did not explode in her face. Another near miss.

At 9:30 they were finally able to crawl out of the building on a fireman's ladder. Had Liz been out at the service window where she normally worked, where over twenty people died, and not back among the file cartons and shelves in the stockroom. . . . The ultimate near miss.

Some say it's luck. Others insist that although for His own inscrutable purposes, God allowed some to die, He also redirected circumstances now and then, here and there, to spare many. People whose lives were saved by some strange little twist vastly outnumber the dead.

One of the strangest turn of events is the story of Tom Hawthorne and Ken Harvey. They weren't just buddies, they were soul mates. They and their wives enjoyed a close social friendship, and often spent hours exploring questions arising from their Bible reading. Tom, at age fifty-two, had read the Bible many times, but in chunks—never straight through cover to cover. He made that his '95 goal.

Tuesday evening, Tom fell off his rickety ladder pruning branches, leaving him bruised and, as he called it, "all stove up." Might Ken go along with him to the Social Security office tomorrow morning? Tom, a union official, was going to try to help a man with glaucoma qualify for assistance. Ken was still in one piece and not on pain meds; Ken could really be of assistance. Afterward, maybe Ken would bring his ladder by and help finish the pruning.

Sure! Ken was happy to.

Later that night, Tom told Ken's answering machine, "Hope your ladder works. See you tomorrow."

At 7:10 the next morning, Ken called and offered to do the driving. Tom insisted they stick to the original plan; he would drive, and he'd come get his pal at 8:30.

But Tom never showed.

Tom Hawthorne had been adamant in sticking to their original plan—pick Ken up and go to the Murrah building together. Why in the world did he change his mind and go to the Murrah building *alone* that morning? . . . Without calling to say what he was doing? Without so much as mentioning to his wife when he kissed her good-bye that he wasn't going to take Ken along after all? We'll never know. Ken Harvey is still alive. Rescuers retrieved Tom's body from the wreckage the next Monday. His goal to read the Bible through in '95 didn't matter anymore. He is with the Author.

You've already heard some stories like these in Chapter Two and throughout the book. And there are fourteen more of these tales in Appendix C of this book. And that's only the ones we could quickly verify.

Among these survivors, two universal responses came, usually within hours or days: "Why me?" or "Why not me?" as the situation warranted, and also a reaction called *survivor guilt*: "I don't deserve to live when all these others died."

Liz Thomas said, "That first night I just cried. I was sure I didn't deserve to live. I had a lot of guilt feelings. All I could think about was my coworkers. I wanted to find out about everybody. When I got out of that building and saw it, I really thought we were the only ones who could have gotten out alive. It really scared me.

"Out of sixty-one employees, I believe we had fifty-three on duty that day, and we lost sixteen. The toll could have been so much higher if it weren't for the emergency exit close by, and the way our office is located on the first floor.

"I didn't deserve to live. None of us do. But He had His hand on me and the rest of the people who got out. We don't know why we were spared, but we were.

"I'm not angry with God, but I keep asking Him, 'Why? Why did this have to happen to us? To the children?'"

Why Me?

Why me?

The callous response is, "Why not you?"

It hardly answers the question.

Related to that is the question, "Why my friend? He was such a loving servant of God. Why would He take that person?"

Robert Wise, the first chaplain in the temporary morgue at the First Methodist Church in Oklahoma City, has pondered this question as many other OKC residents have. In fact, Wise has been struggling with this question for most of his ministry and is the author of two books and numerous articles on the subject.

221

Dr. Wise's response was swift and to the point: "There is no universally satisfactory answer to this question."

He points out that the issue can be answered mechanically and scientifically but not theologically or philosophically in a meaningful or satisfying manner. Factually, we live in a world governed by strict laws of physics, biology, and physiology. Nature is quite indifferent about the consequences of violating these dynamics. If we stand in the path of a deadly projectile, there is no reprieve when the impact comes. Should we be standing one foot to the left or right, we will be unharmed. The results of violating nature's laws are not random or discriminate.

Does this mean that survivors are the happy recipients of good luck, fate, or a fortunate accident of momentary location? Wise says no. The Deists, those who deny the interference of God with the laws of the universe, are wrong. The universe doesn't operate like a clock that Divinity winds up to run alone without His concern or oversight. So we are faced with a paradox.

Scripture is clear God *does* intervene and is involved in history. We live only by and because of His grace. Survivors *always* are the recipients of His blessing. Ask Liz Thomas. She says, "God saved me. He just did."

Liz and other survivors can rejoice in the purpose God still has for them. (This includes everyone who wakes up every morning.) We simply cannot compare our survival with anyone else's demise.

The issue is no longer what happened but what we will make of our survival. Everyone is seeking a universal formula to explain calamities and allow us to sleep more easily in a broken and fallen world. Take our attitude toward death and adversity in America. Somehow, we're supposed to be above all that nasty stuff—or at least insulated from it. We refuse to think about or talk about our own mortality. Death is the ultimate embarrassment. When things go wrong, sue someone to ease the hurt. It's surely someone's fault. When death comes to us, we are shocked and dismayed. (Dick Fenstermacher reminded those at the mayor's prayer breakfast right before the bombing, the death rate is still 100 percent.) We can't believe it would happen to *us*.

Why are some people so certain God acted on their behalf while others have no point of reference for such talk? What makes the difference?

While Robert Wise recognizes the difficulty of explaining the "why's" of tragedy, he has no hesitancy in proclaiming God's power to intervene. He witnessed the promise during the bombing.

Wise reports: "Within a half hour CNN picked up the story and from halfway across the United States, my daughter Traci first realized the possible implications for our family. Not until she called from Modesto, California, did it occur to me my thirty-three-year-old son, Tate, might be near the explosion. An attorney, he usually tried cases in the County Court House blocks away from the blast. However, at the moment of the explosion, Tate was presenting a case in the Federal Court House directly behind the Murrah building."

Robert Wise begins each day praying silently for approximately an hour. Part of this time is spent interceding for each of his four grown children. He asks God to cover them and their families with His protection. As always he prayed on the morning of April 19, 1995.

At 9:01, Tate was waiting in the judge's chambers and was looking out the window, surveying the business district. Thirty seconds before the blast, he turned around to face the judge. At the moment of impact the window shattered, filling his hair, coat, and pants with glass. The ceiling fell in on the secretary. A few minutes later Tate walked out of the building with only a few cuts on his neck. If Tate had still been looking out the window, his face and eyes would have been filled with glass.

Does prayer make a difference? Tate Wise would appear to be *prima facie* evidence. We asked Reverend Wise to give us further insight into how prayer operates in our modern secular world. The following is his perception of the seeming contradictions between the absence and intervention of God:

"Cause and effect can be explained on three levels or dimensions. Each tier has its own perspective and rationale for why things happen. Most people only recognize the existence of one or at the most two of the possibilities.

"Level one is the world of random happenings. We have already acknowledged the natural realm explored and dissected by science. On this plane no connection or relationship to God seems to exist. Divinity either doesn't act or at least make any difference. Every event is understood purely in terms of physical or biological process.

"The novelist John Steinbeck called his perspective 'non-teleological.' Steinbeck saw no meaning in nature. Life is one series of accidents that follow each other without design or meaning. People with his perspective don't believe we can make sense out of what happens to us. Good or bad are human evaluations tacked on to nature. Their standard response to tragedy is, 'Stuff happens.'

"At the other end of the scale, *level three is God's world, the realm of absolutes.* The purposes and designs of the heavenly Father prevail in human affairs. History and destiny, time and eternity intersect on this plane. God does as God chooses according to His design.

"The creation account in Genesis is a level-three story. The call of Abraham from Ur into a covenant with God can only be understood from this perspective. The supreme example of absolute intervention is the resurrection of Jesus on Easter morning. The answer to the inextricable and un-solvable is a simple 'because.'

"If we only use these two vantage points to explain why some survive while others perish, we are forced to extreme conclusions. The world is filled with nonsense because God either does everything or nothing. Special people seem to get favors but most of us apparently don't make the team. Such thinking tends to produce either athe-ists or fanatics.

"Fortunately Scripture suggests a middle ground. *Level one and three are separated by a realm where the randomness of nature and the absolutes of God meet. In this dimension prayer operates and makes a difference.* The Holy Spirit moves and people are touched and energized.

"The area appears cloudy and imprecise to the mind's eye. Scripture offers only broad guidelines rather than formulas and algebraic equations. We have to think with a different logic. Paradox best explains how this dimension operates. The key word is not *because* but *if.*

"*If* people pray, God hears. *If* we listen to the Holy Spirit, divine dirction is given. *When* inter-cessors pray, divine power is released and chan-neled. God's love is focused on human need when the petitions of the faithful ascend. In the 'King-dom of If' faithful obedience to the Word of God makes a real cause-and-effect difference.

"'If' is a crucial concept for farmers. Wheat doesn't grow if seeds aren't planted. If they don't fertilize and pay attention to the seasons, crops don't prosper. Is this principal not equally true on a spiritual plane? Some things don't happen because we didn't pray. Some things happen because we pray."

The sun's rays are available every day but a magnifying glass can focus the heat and create fire that wouldn't exist otherwise. God's love is always constant but prayer concentrates the application of divine grace.

Robert Wise relates, "Bob Moore, a dear friend, recently died from bone cancer, one of the most painful of diseases. People across America prayed for his recovery. To the total surprise of his doctors and family, the last weeks of his life were completely without pain. The absence of excruciating suffering is a singular miracle. Prayer *did* make a difference."

Because the "if factor" isn't examinable or observable, there is always an unpredictable quality to what God does. As the apostle Paul observed, we "only see through a glass dimly."[2] We must walk by trust. We need faith, not a formula.

Did prayer, faith, and the intervention of God have something to do with why some people survived? Without making any comment whatsoever on those who perished, we can absolutely affirm the promise of Scripture was fulfilled for many of the survivors.

What Can We Conclude?

Wise has identified four explanations for why some lived when others died. A few answers recognize the intervention of God, others don't. Here are the options:

1. Some victims just happened to be at the wrong place at the wrong time.

2. God intervened either by saving or taking the person for their own good and His purpose. For centuries Christians and Jews have recognized King Solomon's answer to the question of why some live and others die: "To everything there is a season, a time for every purpose under heaven: A time to be born, and a time to die." [3]

3. Prayer and faith brought spiritual intervention, influencing cause and effect.

4. No complete explanation is possible because the factors are too complex and transcendent for anyone to fully grasp.

Which alternative is correct? Perhaps we don't have to make a choice. They are all possibilities. Each answer has an application for someone. Only God and the individual can make the right application.

The best hope we have is to recover and quest after the particular meaning latent in our individual lives. We can't explain for "them"; we must answer for ourselves.

Relief is found by turning the "why" into a "what." What can I do with my life today and tomorrow? The poignant movie *Braveheart* about Scotland's quest for freedom presents the inescapable issue. We are all going to die. The question is *how* are we going to live?

This is the answer Liz Thomas found: "I personally feel my life is very changed. Now what I want to do is reach out to people and try to share God with them because God saved me. He just did.

"I feel I can do this by telling my story and being a witness. A lot of people are trying to handle this on their own. When it's something of this magnitude, you just can't. You have to look to God. Let Him handle your grief, your sorrow, your pain.

"The whole experience has convinced me that every day should be lived to the fullest. With family, friends, coworkers—mend your fences before it's too late."

The message of this chapter can be summed up with a parable.

A Parable of God's Perspective

A rabbi told this at a memorial on an anniversary of the Holocaust:

The Archangel Michael approached God, absolutely aghast, and pointed toward Earth. "Shaddai, what can You be thinking of? Look what Satan is setting into motion down there!"

"Give the devil his due, there's no one better at creating a tragedy like that one."

"But Shaddai . . . your people . . . your poor people . . ."

"My people have always had the freedom to choose good or evil. You above all should know that. You take them enough warning messages."

"But these people have no choice. Evil is being thrust upon them!"

"Now, Michael, you know what I've always said about the blood of innocents. Have I ever let it go unavenged?"

"No, Shaddai, never. But the suffering! "

"Tchsh! Watch down there! Look at My servant Levi."

"That one? Plain little man. Unassuming. He's never given You a moment's trouble that I remember."

"Ah, Michael, you should hear his prayers! Simple prayers from an aching heart. Now watch this part. Watch! See how he is triumphing over evil? Glorifying Me! Isn't he magnificent?"

"He looks nearly dead to me. Why didn't You stop this? What would—"

"Michael, Michael, Michael. You ask too many questions. Go down and get him. I'll arrange the party."

CHAPTER THIRTEEN

Afterglow

JOANN THOMPSON, WIDOWED WHEN THE bomb took Michael, was never quite sure what her eldest son, twelve-year-old Brett, was going to come up with. And with the loss of his father so fresh at the memorial service that April 23, she really didn't know what he might say. The kid could be downright profound, or he could come up with something totally stupid. He did a lot of both.

So she experienced just a little apprehension when, after the service, President and Mrs. Clinton moved out among the families of those lost and missing. And here they came this way.

Should she worry? Brett grasped the president's hand in a manly shake and said, "It's a true honor to meet you, sir. This is a tribute to my father. Thank you for coming."

That's not the half of it. When they were about to be introduced, the president said to Brett, "Son, you don't even have to tell me who you are. I've read all about you. . . . I'm proud of you."

The Aftermath

Like Brett, thousands of people in Oklahoma not only rose to the occasion but surpassed anyone's expectations. The reverberations of that bomb, and the pun is intended, will echo for years in many good ways as well as bad.

For Good

A short while after the bombing, Dr. Bryan Farha, chairman of Oklahoma City University's Department of Counseling Psychology, traveled to the American Counseling Association's national conference in Denver. In conferences past, Oklahoma had been considered sort of the "country bumpkin cousin," good for a laugh but not to be taken too seriously. This year, Farha found there something for Oklahoma that he hadn't seen before. Respect.

The conference representatives told him they will provide free counseling for people outside Oklahoma who were emotionally affected by the bombing. The Association recognized, and rightly so, that Oklahoma has the resources and expertise to take care of her own.[1]

Oklahoma's self-respect and the respect in which she is held from outside have risen tremendously. Oklahoma has not changed. She has only shown what she's really about. Even her own citizens had not realized how splendid a state she is.

The Oklahoma City Standard is what it's called; it's the new level to which search and rescue support has risen, as mentioned before. That standard was established by a community and a state that organized virtually instantly to provide every need for both outsiders and locals in the rescue and retrieval effort. No bureaucratic hemming and hawing. The decisiveness began with ordinary citizens scrambling up into the wreckage to save lives. It continued as churches and the restaurant association made hard decisions fast and then stuck with them. It rolled on with the governor's firm hand at the helm, the public safety officers working in concert, and the medical community providing everyone the finest of care and relegating red tape to the back burner where it belonged.

What a time it was!

Perhaps for the first time, Oklahomans realized that they can work together efficiently. It's no small lesson. We'd never thought much about it before.

On June 20, The First United Methodist Church, that brick church with the dome right across from the Murrah site, announced plans for an open-air chapel. The announcement told the world that the Heartland Chapel will be available to anyone at any time. The altar is built of stones broken from the church by the blast and features a special box for prayer requests.

Some of the funds for the chapel were raised from members of the church.

But the project, essentially, was made possible by a substantial gift from the Explosion Fund of the Jewish Federation in Oklahoma City. That's truly working together in the Heartland. Another miracle to rise out of the ashes.

The Lessons

The good and the bad of the tragedy will reach their maximum meaning if they are accompanied by learning. And there is much to learn. It is most constructive to move from "Why did this happen to me?" into "What can I gain from this?" It is, in fact, a very positive sign of healing—a step many Oklahomans have already begun to take.

Soon after the bombing a gang member called a local radio show to ask his fellow gang members, "Why should we be appalled at this when we are involved in senseless violence every day?" That day he hung up his gang colors and challenged others to do the same!

By glorifying God in the face of Satan, by seizing the good, and by learning from the experience, we thwart the evil.

Some Oklahomans are experiencing another miracle, the one which is the greatest miracle of all.

The Greatest Miracle of All

Forgiveness.

Forgive the person or persons who killed the little children? The person who killed our husbands and wives, sons and daughters, sisters and brothers, cousins and friends? The person who destroyed our city—and more than that, our innocence?

Although forgiveness is central to healing, forgiveness is a factor of the aftermath. While we still sought survivors, and as workers dug for the last of the bodies, few could think about forgiveness, let alone seriously consider it. We needed some distance, some perspective, some closure.

Soon after the blast, the *Daily Oklahoman* quoted survivor Randy Ledger regarding his difficulty with forgiveness. No wonder. He was trussed into a hospital bed, unable to speak or move his head, communicating by pencil on paper he could not look at. He could not see his family at his bedside, let alone the healing in the distance.

The time required may vary, but in willing hearts, forgiveness eventually becomes possible. It may tiptoe in virtually unbidden; it may enter under great duress. Forced. Either way, it applies the final balm of healing, and nothing else can do what forgiveness does.

Those who recognize God as supreme understand that forgiveness is His will. For them, doing His will is even more important than healing. But how? It helps to understand how forgiveness works and what it does.

Forgiving Is Not Forgetting

"I can never forget." So many survivors and next-of-kin say that. News media quoted them on site, and they still say it.

Of course they cannot! No one suggests that they ought.

The officer who placed tiny Baylee Almon into the firefighter's arms, the firefighter who carried her to a waiting aid van, the medical officer in the van who snuggled her so that she would not die alone—can any of them ever forget her? Hardly! Her mother certainly cannot. Everywhere she looks, there is the image of her child in the firefighter's arms. Each of these people, in his or her own way, must face the issue of forgiving an agent of Satan. Humanly impossible.

"Forgive and forget" is a colloquialism perpetuated, no doubt, by offenders. Naturally they want the people they offend to forget the offense. However, the offendees then resist forgiving because it has been tied to forgetting and they know they can't do that.

So dismiss the old saw, "Forgive and forget." It's not true, it doesn't work, and it gets in the way of healing. Its replacement doesn't roll off the tongue as alliteratively, but here is the reality: "Forgive even though you remember."

Big Offenses Are Harder to Forgive

Everyone more or less knows that, but there's a hooker here: In human terms, the size of the offense is strictly relative, but not to God.

Says a friend, "I've always been a horse nut, and I had a collection of horse figurines when I was a kid. One day my mom broke my favorite while she was dusting. The thing was worth, at most, a couple of bucks, and it was an accident, but I had a terrible time forgiving her. It meant so much to me."

Not a big thing, but *it meant so much to me*. Some persons lost relatively little in the bombing, objectively speaking, but they perceive their loss as great. They may have as much trouble forgiving as those who suffered horrible loss by any person's measure. All may take comfort in the fact that God doesn't grade loss and injustice on a sliding scale. Injustice is injustice. Any sin is sin.

Early in the rescue effort, when passions and adrenaline were running high, a truck driver hailed David Brinkley, the chaplain. "If the guy who did this confessed to God and asked forgiveness, would he be forgiven?" asked the trucker.

"Yes."

"And go to heaven?"

The chaplain, a Christian, answered, "Yes, if he repented and accepted Christ's sacrifice as the payment for his sins."

That answer provides comfort, not dismay. Every person has committed wrongs. Every person. In Christian theology, no person deserves heaven. Bomber and gossiper, murderer and the uncharitable—all fall short. Christian belief further states that a wrong is a wrong, whether it be big or small, because it is an offense to God. If God were selective about forgiving wrongs when forgiveness was genuinely asked, who could know where the line would be drawn by that divine finger? This offense is forgiven but that one is not. "Am I really forgiven? Was my offense too big to make the cut?" We don't have to worry about it.

Another point that often seems murky is the purpose of forgiveness.

Forgiving Does Not Benefit the Offender Primarily

Throughout this book we have told stories of people who were delivered miraculously out of death. We've been describing the horrors which the rescue workers went through. We've mentioned person after person who suffered terrible loss. We've talked about the immense burden the chaplains voluntarily assumed, suffering the shock and outrage of the people in their care as they comforted them. We've delighted in telling you about the many, many "ordinary" people who performed extraordinary deeds of courage and tenacity.

Each of these persons and thousands more—all of Oklahoma and America, individually and corporately—must forgive, not so much for the sake of the perpetrator as for themselves. The act of forgiving is a healing act for the forgiver even more so than for the offender. So far as the forgiver's benefit is concerned, it does not really matter whether the offender accepts the forgiveness or not. Offering forgiveness is the key.

The offer must, of course, be genuine.

Sherman Catalon, the assistant building manager who lived through the bombing, phrases it very well:

"This is what gives me peace today: God is the one to judge. It is not for me to judge. I have no hatred for anyone. I see the hate and anger that created this situation and know there has been enough destruction."

Enough indeed. He is so right.

Forgiving Is Usually Not Humanly Possible

When the pope of the Catholic church visited the man who had tried to assassinate him, it was not an act of show for the press. The Pope was delivering his message of forgiveness in person.

"Well," a survivor might say, "you expect the Pope to do that. He's supposed to be as perfectly pure and pious as possible. Besides, he's also supposed to provide his followers with a perfect example. So sure, he's going to march into that jail and say, 'I forgive you.'

"Hey. I'm not a pope. I'm not perfect and pure and pious. I can't handle it. Sorry."

Neither could Corrie ten Boom when she came face to face with a former Nazi who would have been directly responsible for her saintly sister Betsy's death. Many have heard her dramatic narrative of the incident. She could not forgive in her own strength, and this was one of the strongest, most eloquent Christians the world has ever seen.

And right there lies the key to true spiritual strength. She stepped back, spiritually speaking, and let God do for her what she could not do herself. She forgave that man—not through her own ability but through her God's.

"I cannot forgive you in my own strength. I forgive you in the (name) (strength) of (God) (Jesus Christ)."

That is real strength.

Would someone who lost a loved one be able to forgive in his or her own strength, with time? Possibly. But they need respite and healing now, not eventually. More importantly, when Jesus taught us to pray the Lord's Prayer—Forgive us our trespasses as we forgive those who trespass against us—He linked the vertical to the horizontal. A person's lack of forgiveness will sour any hope of a close personal relationship with God. And most of us need that right now also. Forgiveness has been possible for some Oklahomans.

One Woman's Story of Forgiveness

Seven years less a day before Bob Westberry died in the Murrah building, his eldest daughter died—April 20, 1988. Before he went to work on the morning of the nineteenth, he and his wife, Tillie, talked about her awhile, since tomorrow would be the anniversary of her death.

It took workers nearly four days to identify Bob's remains, using dental records and finger-prints the medical examiner lifted off Bob's Bible. Tillie wanted Bob, and eventually herself, interred beside their deceased daughter in Parkland Memorial Gardens. The cemetery found two plots directly above the daughter's.

Everyone who knew the situation at Parkland agreed, finding plots together like that constituted a miracle.

Tillie Westberry calculates that her husband Bob's desk stood about thirty feet from the blast. Bob was the supervising agent in charge of the Defense Department. Even so godly a woman could have a little private hatred. She has none. She understands the situation. "Because we are all born in sin, I don't have any hate, not even toward [the perpetrator]. We all need the grace of God."

It's not just bravado on her part, or a more-pious-than-thou attitude. Few Christians are more solidly anchored in the faith than Tillie West-berry and few are as humble about it. She under-stands that we all stand in need of God's mercy, and all share an equal chance of obtaining it.

Tillie Westberry and Sherman Catalon have already forgiven the bomber. That these people can forgive is the greatest miracle of all and the major lesson for the rest of us. Yet there are still other lessons from these people on the front line.

Other Lessons from the People on the Front Line

A thousand different people who came into contact with Oklahoma City's little piece of hell repeated the same things again and again. There's nothing new in them; they are basic things. We've heard them all a hundred times or more. As a result, we've ceased to hear their message and their simple eloquence. Listen one more time to the voices of people who know:

- A mother who lost her children: "I'd give anything to be able to read for the kids."
- Robyn Parent, as she faced the loss of her left eye: "If I lose my sight, it's nothing; I still have my life."
- Priscilla Salyers, whose story we told earlier: "God was on the back burner of my life. He certainly got my attention." She has a new boldness to witness for God.

- Tonya Rowlett, who was running late and therefore her two-year-old son Chance was not in the day-care center at the Murrah building that morning, says: "Yesterday, I just kept hugging him and saying, 'Chance, I love you so much.' This morning he patted my face and said, 'Momma, I love you so much.'"[2]
- Tillie Westberry, who lost her husband, Bob: "If I left any advice for anyone, before you ever leave or say good-bye to your wife, partner, or children, never leave mad. Always be careful of the last things you say. I am thankful I have no regret."

The Lessons Applied

What little things would you change, given the chance? What ought to be important to you but it has been shouldered aside by the immediate? Perhaps it's time to reassess priorities and then act upon that reassessment.

We encourage you to become more involved in life now, and to live a life without regrets. Well, all right—fewer regrets!

The gang member makes an excellent point as well. Every tragedy is a tragedy. Size is relative.

The Ultimate Lesson

There is one more way in which you can give the tragedy a positive meaning, and it is the most important way of all. Choose God.

We talked earlier about how Lucifer disguises himself as what he once was, an angel of light, and thereby misleads millions.

Somebody out there bought Satan's lies and brought catastrophe to downtown Oklahoma City. A sad, terrible choice. And yet thousands of people in Oklahoma City made a choice also: They chose God.

How can you tell the difference, if Lucifer looks so good? How do you know you're choosing God?

Love. Satan cannot love. God *is* love.

Oklahoma City proved that. . . .

Where was God at 9:02 A.M.?

Many Oklahomans answer that question by saying, "He walked among us."

Epilogue

NINE THOUSAND PEOPLE—RESCUERS, families of victims, survivors, and thousands of other hurting Oklahomans—attended an Evening of Encouragement in the State Fair Arena a few short weeks after the bombing. Sandi Patti provided music and comedian/singer Mark Lowry contributed his wit and songs. Author and speaker Max Lucado offered beautiful illustrations of God's love for His people of Oklahoma, and for you—for all His children, regardless of the nature of the tragedy in their lives.

Because of the profound relevancy of Mr. Lucado's remarks, we close our book with them. May they provide encouragement for you in your dark hour.

Max Lucado:

Hidden in the meadow grass and weeds, the whippoorwill, a dark, squat bird a little chubbier than a robin, sings a haunting, plaintive "Hoo hoo h-wee?" early and late in the day. (You out West know its close cousin the Poor-Will.)

The whippoorwill, some people claim, serves a purpose with its call. Its task, so 'tis said, is to anticipate what is yet to come. Its song signals to the dawn and heralds the coming dusk. Within each of us, deep down, where ears can't hear, the whippoorwill gives voice to our hungers and discontent, and it sings a song of eternity.

Perched in time, that song within us sings of a timeless place. Shrouded in pain, we sing of a painless place. Living in faceless gray, we anticipate a golden place. And there is no time that the whippoorwill sings more loudly and boldly than he does at a time of tragedy.

"It's not right!" we say, "that innocents suffer!
"It's not right that the hungry go unfed. . . .
"That injustice permeates the land.
"It's not right!"

But before we shake a fist at heaven, let's pause for a moment here: How do we know it's not right? Who told us it's not right? Where did we get that impression? Could it be that this dissatisfaction, this longing, is God's gift to us, lest we fail to understand that things are not right *in this world*?

When you cry out, "It's not right!" the response from heaven is, "You are correct. It's not right!"

We must know that it's not right that God became flesh, lived on this earth, slept on hard

246

ground. . . . *that the King of Kings was stapled to a Roman cross. When we cry out, He agrees with us. He knows.*

Could it be that this voice, this cry of dissatisfaction from the whippoorwill, is not something to avoid, but rather something to listen to? God has given us a healthy discontent to remind us that we are not home yet. The reason we know it's not right is because God placed within us a homing device, if you would, that registers when wrong comes. The greatest tragedy we face is failing to hear that voice, is feeling that it is right when it's not.

Picture a fish cast up on the beach. Its fins are getting crispy in the sun. What does that fish need? I look at the fish, it looks at me, and I know it's hurting.

"I know what this fish needs!" I run down to the bank, get a lot of money, and dump it on top of the fish. I ask the fish, "Does that help?"

"No. It doesn't help."

I hurry down to the store, buy a martini, and pour it on the fish. "Does that help?"

"Well, it's not bad. But it doesn't seem right."

I try a Playfish *magazine.* "How's that?"

The fish flops through it with his one good eye. "Nice. But that's still not it."

I know! I wade out into the water and get a she fish, and drop it beside the he fish.

About this time, you're saying, "Lucado, is everybody in Texas that dumb? If you want a fish to get better, you have to pick it up and put it back in the water. It will never be content, no matter what you do, until you put it back in the water where it belongs."

And we won't be content either until we reach where we belong. We're not made for this planet; we're fish out of water. Oh, sure, it's all right now and then, but there are times when the beach is awfully rocky, and the air is awfully stale.

It was just for that reason, on the night before the greatest tragedy, that Jesus told His own, "Don't let your hearts be troubled. Trust in God. Trust also in Me. In My father's house are many mansions. If that weren't so, I would not have said it. I am going there to prepare a place for you."

Some weeks ago at a party at our house, our youngest daughter fell asleep on the couch downstairs. So I did what fathers have been doing forever; I carried her upstairs to her room and put her in her bed. Now why did I do that? Was it a cruel act? Of course not. She might have rested all right down there on the couch, but I had this room prepared for her upstairs. You see, it's not out of cruelty but out of love that the father takes his child upstairs so that child can rest well in a room prepared.

She and her sisters like to be together. What if her two older sisters objected? "Please don't take Sara upstairs."

I would have understood their objections. "I understand. But what I have for her up there is so *much better. And it won't be long until you'll go up there to be with her too."*[1]

Max Lucado's message has particular significance for Oklahomans. Many of them are like Sara's sisters. They know their loved ones are in a better place. Yet they naturally long for their sons and daughters, husbands and wives, relatives and friends who are no longer with them.

In Appendix A we issue a challenge for those who wish to accept it. First, we list those 168 who died in Oklahoma City. Then we present our challenge: If you believe in the power of prayer, we suggest that you choose a name and commit that person's family and friends to God's care for the next year.

Prayer makes a difference. We in Oklahoma City have found that to be so.

APPENDIX A

Your Assignment, If You Choose to Accept It

PAIN AND HEALING DO NOT NEATLY resolve themselves the moment the hoopla dies down. They persist for years, abating, it sometimes seems, at a snail's pace. Here is a listing of those who died. They left behind family, friends, and bewildered acquaintances who regretted not knowing them better.

We invite—nay, we challenge—you the reader to choose a name and commit to prayer for the next calendar year the halo of friends and family around that deceased person. The living will continue to need spiritual support long after the Murrah building tragedy melts into history.

(Abbreviations: AK America's Kids Day Care Center; DD Defense Department; DEA Drug Enforcement Agency; FECU Federal Employees Credit Union; FHWA Federal Highway Administration; GSA General Services Administration; HUD Housing and Urban Development; SS Secret Service (agents and employees); SSA Social Security Administration; USA United States Army (both enlisted and civilian employees); USCS United States Customs Service; USDA United States Department of Agriculture; USDT United States Department of Transportation; USMC United States Marine Corps.)

Aleman, Lucio Jr. 33. FHWA. Safety engineer.
Allen, Richard A. 46. SSA. Claims.
Allen, Ted L. 48. HUD. Community planner.
Alexander, Teresa. 33.
Almon, Baylee. 1. AK.
Althouse, Diane E. 45. HUD. Loan manager.
Anderson, Rebecca. 37. The nurse who came running to help.
Argo, Pamela. 36.
Avery, Saundra. 34. SSA. Clerk.
Avillanoza, Peter. 56. HUD. Fair housing, EO director.
Battle, Calvin. 62.
Battle, Peola. 56.
Bell, Danielle. 1. AK.
Biddy, Oleta. 54. SSA. Service representative.
Bland, Shelly. 25. DEA. Asset Forfeiture Specialist.
Blanton, Andrea. 33. HUD. Secretary.
Bloomer, Olen. 61. USDA. Budget.
Bolden, Lola. 40. Sgt. FC, USA Recruiting.
Boles, James. 51. USDA. Administrative officer.
Bolte, Mark. 27. FHWA. Highway engineer.
Booker, Cassandra. 25.

Bowers, Carol. 53. SSA. Supervisor.
Bradley, Peachlyn. 3.
Brady, Woodrow. 41.
Brown, Cynthia. 26. SS. Agent.
Broxterman, Paul. HUD. 43.
Bruce, Gabreon. 3 mo.
Burgess, Kimberly. 29. FECU.
Burkett, David. 47. HUD.
Burns, Donald Sr. 63. HUD. Construction analyst.
Carr, Karen. 32. USA. Recruiting.
Carillo, Michael. 44. FHWA.
Chafey, Rona. 35. DEA. Assigned from Sheriff's office.
Chavez, Zackary. 3. AK.
Chipman, Robert. 51. OK Water Resources Board
  (across street).
Clark, Kimberly. 39. HUD.
Clark, Margaret. 42. USDA. Veterinary medical officer.
Cooper, Anthony II. 2. AK.
Cooper, Antonio. 6 mo. AK.
Cooper, Dana. 24. AK. Director.
Cottingham, Harley. 46. DD. Agent.
Cousins, Kim. 33. HUD.
Coverdale, Aaron. 5. AK.
Coverdale, Elijah. 2. AK.
Coyne, Jaci. 1. AK.
Cregan, Kathy. 60. SSA. Claims.
Cummins, Richard. 55. USDA. Investigator.
Curry, Steven. 44. GSA. Inspector.
Daniels, Brenda. 42. AK. Caregiver.
Davis, Benjamin. Sgt., USMC.
Day, Diana. 38. HUD.
DeMaster, Peter. 44. DD. Agent.
Deveroux, Castine. 49. HUD. Clerk.

Driver, Sheila. 28.

Eaves, Tylor. 8 mo. AK.

Eckles, Ashley. 4.

Ferrell, Susan. 37. HUD. Attorney.

Fields, Carroll. 48. DEA.

Finley, Katherine. 44. FECU.

Fisher, Judy. 45. HUD.

Florence, Linda. 43. HUD.

Fritzler, Donald. 64.

Fritzler, Mary. 57.

Garrett, Tevin. 1. AK.

Garrison, Laura. 61.

Genzer, Jamie. 32. FECU. Loan officer.

Goodson, Margaret. 54. SSA. Claims.

Gottshall, Kevin. 6 mo. AK.

Griffin, Ethel. 55. SSA. Claims.

Guiles, Colleen, 59. HUD. Senior underwriter.

Guzman, Randolph. 28. Capt., USMC.

Hammons, Cheryl. 44.

Harding, Ronald. 55. SSA. Claims.

Hawthorne, Thomas Sr. 52.

Higginbottom, Doris. 44. USDA. Purchasing.

Hightower, Anita. 27. Job Corps. In restaurant
across street.

Hodges, Gene Jr. 54. HUD. Evaluation supervisor.

Holland, Peggy. 37. USA Recruiting.
Computer specialist.

Housley, Linda. 53. FECU.

Howard, George. 45. HUD.

Howell, Wanda. 34. AK. Teacher/caregiver.

Huff, Robbin. 37. FECU. Loan officer.

Hurlburt, Dr. Charles. 73. Dentist.

Hurlburt, Jean. 67. Wife of Charles.

Ice, Paul. 42. USCS. Agent.

Jenkins, Christi. 32. FECU.

Johnson, Norma. 62. DD. Executive secretary.

Johnson, Raymond. 59. SSA. Volunteer.

Jones, Larry. 46. FHWA. Computer specialist.

Justes, Alvin. 54. Vietnam Veteran.

Kennedy, Blake. 1. AK.

Khalil, Carole. 50. USDA.

Koelsch, Valerie. 33. FECU.

Kreymborg, Carolyn. 57. HUD. Loan management.

Lauderdale, Teresa. 41. HUD. Realty specialist.

Leinen, Kathy. 47. FECU.

Lenz, Carrie. 26. DEA, on contract.

Leonard, Donald. 50. SS. Agent.

Levy, Lakesha. 21. USAF, Airman FC.

London, Dominique. 2. AK.

Long, Rheta. 60. USDA. Secretary.

Loudenslager, Michael. 48. GSA.

Luster, Aurelia. 43.

Luster, Robert Jr. 45.

Maroney, Mickael. 50. SS. Agent.

Martin, James. 34. FHWA. Highway engineer.

Martinez, Gilberto. 35. Assemblies of God pastor.

McCarthy, James. 53. HUD.

McCullough, Kenneth. 36. DEA. Agent.

McGonnell, Betsy. 47. HUD.

McKinney, Linda. 47. SS. Office manager.

McRaven, Cartney. USAF, Airman FC.

Medearis, Claude, 41. USCS. Agent.

Meek, Claudette. 43. FECU.

Merrell, Frankie. 23. FECU.

Miller, Derwin. 27.

Mitchell, Eula. 64.

Moss, John III. 51. USA Recruiting.

Nix, Patricia. 47. HUD.

Parker, Jerry. 45. FHWA. Engineer.

Randolph, Jill. 27. FECU

Reeder, Michelle. 33. FHWA.

Rees, Terry. 41. HUD, acting director of housing.

Rentie, Mary. 39. HUD.

Reyes, Antonio. 55. HUD. Fair housing.

Ridley, Kathryn. 24. Job Corps. In Athenian, across the street.

Rigney, Trudy, 31. OK Water Resources Board, across the street.

Ritter, Claudine. 48. FECU.

Rosas, Christy. 22. FECU.

Sanders, Sonja. 27. FECU.

Scroggins, Lanny. 46. HUD.

Seidl, Kathy. 39. SS.

Sells, Leora. 57. HUD.

Shepherd, Karan. 27. FECU. Loan officer.

Smith, Chase. 3. AK.

Smith, Colton. 2. AK.

Sohn, Victoria. 36. Master Sgt., USA.

Stewart, John. 51. HUD.

Stratton, Dolores. 51. USA Recruiting.

Tapia, Emilio. 50.

Texter, Victoria. 37. FECU.

Thomas, Charlotte. 43. SSA.

Thompson, Michael. 46. SSA.

Thompson, Virginia. 56. FECU.

Titsworth, Kayla. 3.

Tomlin, Ricky. 46. USDT.

Treanor, LaRue. 56.

Treanor, Luther. 61.

Turner, Larry. 43. DD. Agent.

Valdez, Jules. 50. HUD.

VanEss, John. 67. HUD.

Wade, Johnny. 42. FHWA. Planning and research.

Walker, David. 54. HUD.

Walker, Robert. 52.

Watkins, Wanda. 49. USA.

Weaver, Michael. 45. Attorney.

Welch, Julie. 23. SSA. Claims.

Westberry, Robert. 57. DD. Agent.

Whicher, Alan. 40. SS. Agent.

Whittenberg, Jo Ann. 40. SS. Agent.

Williams, Frances. 48. HUD.

Williams, Scott. 24.

Williams, William Stephen. 42. SSA.

Wilson, Clarence. 49. HUD. Chief Counsel,
    acting manager.

Woodbridge, Ronota. 31. FHWA.

Woodchesnut, Sharon. 47. SSA. Claims.

Worton, Tresia. 28. FECU.

Youngblood, John. 52. FHWA.

More Stories of Love and Encouragement

THERE WERE SO MANY STORIES OF LOVE AND encouragement in Oklahoma we were unable to include every one in the book. Here are yet other stories of God's love expressed through His people.

Comfort to the Rescuers and Victims' Relatives

One of the chaplains, David Brinkley (no relation to the news commentator), offers his recollections: "Right after it happened, when the request for chaplains went out, I responded and went down there. What struck me was all the debris. Building material, of course, but also metal. There were large metal fragments all over.

"The sheriff's deputy recognized me and put me on crowd control near the YMCA. But my law enforcement career ended early and I was soon doing what I came to do. Chaplaincy.

"They needed chaplains at ground zero. Those of us who started working there as chaplains pretty much stayed there. Security is why. A lot of agencies were in there, and they wanted a limited number of faces to be familiar with, so they limited the number of clearances.

"The first thing we did as chaplains, in the middle of the first shift, was give out bananas and bottles of water. No debriefing, no heavy prayer, no intensive one-on-one. But I'm not complaining by any means. Few things are more practical, or less glamorous, than a banana. Part of the grace of God is meeting the need of the moment. That's usually the antithesis of glamour, I've found."

Later David Brinkley comforted victims' relatives. He had his own pain, which grace converted into gifts for others. "I was one of the few who could tell the waiting family members, 'I truly understand how you feel.' My dad was murdered, and it was four days before we found out what happened.

"I worked the eastern perimeter near the morgue, with the homicide detectives who were working with the bodies rescuers pulled out of the pit. I can never forget when they brought the last three children out.

"You know they had to leave a few victims in the rubble until they could bring that dangerous wall down. They dealt with a lot of remorse over that, and feelings of failure. But they set a goal to account for all the children before they quit.

"When the last child was brought out, a worker threw his helmet into the air. 'Thank You, Lord, for letting us meet the goal!'"

The Comfort Given by Passersby

Jay Barnett was directing traffic near ground zero, hours after the blast. Others experienced the adrenaline rush, the macho task, of digging through the debris for survivors. Jay was trying to keep gawkers from playing bumper cars.

Now as an officer, Jay had become more or less accustomed to a lack of appreciation from people. Clouds moved in, the temperature dropped, and here came the rain.

A passerby called to the wet, bedraggled, heart-weary officer, "Want some coffee?"

No need to think twice. "Yeah, I would." Office workers often brought along a thermos. So he assumed the fellow would whip out a cup and bottle.

The fellow had no such thing. He was back in a couple of minutes with coffee, but he had had to go track some down.

"I couldn't believe it. It was the strangest mix of feeling the horror behind me and then feeling the way people rallied to support everybody. The support was almost as unbelievable as the horror."

Jay had just experienced the opening salvo in a phenomenon neither he nor any other police officer in town would ever have dreamt could happen: Citizens began overtly and enthusiastically appreciating their public safety officers.

People smiled and waved to cops. They stopped ambulance drivers on nonemergency runs just to chat, neighborly. They blew kisses to firefighters.

For years, fire departments in the city (not just Oklahoma City; they do this just about everywhere) have been conducting school programs to teach children not to fear firefighters in those scary turnouts. No one wants a small child in a burning structure to see a firefighter and run hide. A grown person in bunkers and a Surviv-Air pack and mask usually scared the kids in spite of the talks and the fire education. Not now. Children came running up for a hug.

And Jay Barnett's experience is not unique.

Andy Kidd, an agent for the state's Alcoholic Beverage Laws Enforcement Commission, was out on loan to the city after the blast, directing traffic. He too was tired and hot. Although he normally worked plainclothes, on this traffic detail he wore the full regalia—blue uniform, body armor, sidearm, cuffs, and all.

It was hot. Really hot. Really, *really* hot. He recalls: "I was thinking to myself, *Boy I'm thirsty.*

"Just then a Red Cross vehicle pulled up. 'Need anything to drink? Coke? Coffee?'

"'I'd really like water.'

"'Here's some water,' and they passed me a liter of bottled tapwater.

"Well, somebody just passing by heard that and came back thirty minutes later with an ice chest of bottled Ozarks drinking water.

"Later I could tell I was starting to get sunburned, and I thought to myself, *I sure wish I'd brought my sunscreen.*

"Someone, a total stranger, pulled up, 'Need anything?'

"'Yeah. Got any sunscreen?'

"'Sure do, Buddy. Here you go.' And they passed it out the window to me.

"'Say, you don't have any sunglasses, do you?'

"'Well, as a matter of fact, we do.'"

More Stories of Those Who Survived

HERE ARE THE FASCINATING STORIES OF those who survived because of some change in routine. Some might call them "near-miss" stories:

Brenda Rodgers

Brenda Rodgers had some ideas she wanted to bounce off her pastor—nothing earth-shaking—and made an appointment to talk to him Monday. Monday got messed up and she tried to cancel, but he suggested moving the appointment to Tuesday afternoon. After they met, she happened to remember an ATM near the church that was geared to take her credit union deposit. It would save her a trip downtown the next morning.

The next morning she was standing at her desk, working on the fourteenth floor of her building six miles from ground zero, when the room rocked. Her secretary shouted, "An explosion downtown!"

Brenda could think of nothing to do except pray. Along with much of the rest of America, she watched the news coverage in shocked sorrow, feeling helpless. Even as the video cameras recorded the devastation of the building which housed her credit union, a building she visited frequently on business, the realization didn't hit her until that afternoon:

Had she not gone ahead with that appointment, and had she not then thought of the ATM machine and made her deposit on late Tuesday afternoon instead, she or her husband would have been standing in the hall, waiting her turn at the counter of the credit union, on Wednesday at 9:02 A.M.

The Window Washers

Window washers were plying their trade up on the twentieth floor of the Regency Towers apartments, hanging out there in bare air on their scaffolding. The blast partially collapsed their scaffolding, but they managed to crawl in a window. They credit their survival at least in part to a four-foot balcony extension which provided limited shielding.

Nick Harris's Son-in-Law

Nick Harris, pastor of First United Methodist, right across from the Murrah building, already described the events that kept him and his sound engineer from their routine taping session Wednesday morning. There is more. Nick's son-in-law, the church's youth minister, happened to be out of his office when his double windows blew in—frames and all—and slammed down across his desk and chair. The associate pastor just happened to be in Enid that morning. And a sales representative who was slated to come by that morning had to cancel. The church lost no personnel, despite the fact that you could throw a stone from the churchyard and hit the Murrah building.

Nick wags his head. "It's a wonder."

Merkel X-Ray Company Workers

Merkel X-ray Co. workers were blown off their chairs. Later, one of them pointed to an office with shattered windows. "Our sales manager had just walked out of this office. It would have killed him if he'd been there."

Glenda McDaniel

Glenda McDaniel and her friend Cyndi usually took their break together at 9:30 A.M. Wednesday morning, just before 9, Cyndi stopped by Glenda's desk. She had to attend a seminar today, and she was late already, so she wouldn't be breaking at 9:30. Glenda happened to be at a good stopping point just then, so she decided to go ahead and break now. At 9:02 she was away, upstairs in the breakroom, when her office was destroyed.

Christopher Nguyen

Little Christopher Nguyen loved to play in water. He splashed and dabbled in it anytime he could get away with it. He was probably pursuing his favorite activity in the rest room when the bomb went off. Burned and comatose, he nonetheless survived. His father, Thu, has no doubt that the protection of that extra rest room wall saved his son's life.[1]

Andy Kidd

Andy Kidd intended to drop by Customs at 9:00 A.M. to meet Paul Ice, the man who died a moment after making eye contact with Priscilla Salyers. Andy and Paul, along with Priscilla Salyers and Ken Dahl, were close friends. Andy was going to give a weapon back to Paul and take him along to Bartlesville on mutual business. Instead, for no real reason whatever, Andy went to his office first. In retrospect, he can't really say why. He usually didn't stop by his office at all; he worked primarily out in the field. There was some little reason. He called the customs office to tell Paul he would be late. The phone rang twice and went dead.[2]

Priscilla Salyers

Priscilla Salyers, who received comfort from a corpse's hand before being pulled out of the wreckage, has her own near-miss tale to tell.

Usually, she arrived at work about 8:30. She would pick up the mail in the first-floor post office at 9 and return to her desk to go through it. Tuesday night, though, a girlfriend called and asked if Priscilla would stop by for coffee in the morning. Priscilla left half an hour early, but the coffee klatch fell through. So she continued on to work, arriving at 8. She picked up the mail and left the first floor around 8:15 instead of at 9 and, as they say, the rest is history.

Nancy Trippett

Nancy Trippett was scheduled to give birth to her firstborn on March 6. Her doctor decided to hold off inducing labor. They induced three days later.

Nancy was home with her husband, James, and her baby, Jennifer, when the bomb went off. Nancy's particular office, the Department of Health and Human Services, was tucked into the southeast corner of the third floor directly beyond the Federal Employees Credit Union.

Three of DHHS's desks were dumped into the pit, but they went down empty. Two of the desks' users happened to be working in a back room and escaped serious injury. The user of the third lost desk, Nancy Trippett, was still out on maternity leave.

Her maternity leave ended April 19, the very day of the bombing. Had they induced labor on schedule as they originally planned, her maternity leave would have ended April 16. She would have been back to work April 17.

Karen Evans

Karen Evans, estranged from her child's father, was going to keep her daughter that week, but little Angela Nelson's dad in Chickasha took the child instead. Angela was safe in another town when the bomb destroyed her day-care center.[3]

Rhonda Reynolds

Like several other parents, Rhonda Reynolds had pulled her girls out of the day-care center a couple of weeks before. At the time of the blast, her children were home in the care of a nanny.

Terry Wilson

Terry Wilson, the head of Customs, had stopped by his doctor's office and was also running late. At 9:02 he had not yet arrived at work.

Kate Worsham

Kate Worsham cancelled a 9 A.M. meeting in the Oklahoma City Social Security office because she had to stay over in Ft. Worth, Texas, on business. Several weeks later, she returned as acting director, replacing the person who died.

A Friend of Jack Poe's

Jack Poe, OKC police chaplain, tells this story: "I got there shortly after the blast. As soon as I could, I went out looking for the beat officer that we knew was in the area. I wanted to make sure we didn't lose him.

"Now this man was the sort of person who keeps his distance. Friendly, helpful, good social skills, but not demonstrative. He didn't have much use for what he called 'touchy-feely.'

"There he was. I spotted him and then he saw me. He hugged me. He kept on hugging me. And hugging me. What was going on here? In a minute, he told me his story:

"'I stop by for coffee there every morning around 9, Jack. Except for this morning. This morning I had car trouble.'

"He just kept hugging me. Hug, hug. Then came the big one:

"'My two grandkids are supposed to be in day care there, but they're both home sick today.'"

267

Floor Statement of Oklahoma Congressman J. C. Watts

HERE IS, IN ITS ESSENCE, THE FLOOR statement delivered to Congress by Congressman J. C. Watts several weeks after the incident.

The tragedy in Oklahoma City is the most horrific act of terrorism and violence ever to have occurred within the borders of this great nation. I've been at the site and I have seen the destruction firsthand. Yesterday I preached at the funeral of my friend, Clarence Wilson.

We lost more than two dozen residents of my district, including an eighteen-month-old child in Chickasha. My heart goes out to all those people. Nothing can replace the loss, and only a lot of time, love, and prayers can begin to heal the wounds. As the father of five healthy, vibrant children, I can't imagine anything worse than losing a child. The sight of the fireman carrying Baylee Almon will be forever etched on my mind.

In the face of tragedy, once again the heart of the nation is shown to be strong and compassionate. The whole country has unified to support us, and the relief efforts have been tremendous. The support for our emergency service people—police, fire, EMSA, FBI— have been overwhelming. This is the most united, coordinated effort we have ever seen. Thank you from the bottom of our collective hearts.

These last few weeks, there have been no Democrats or Republicans, no Black or White, no Brown or Red, no male or female—just all Americans united for a common cause.

If what the perpetrators of this crime meant to send is a message, we have one for them: We will seek you out and make sure you pay for the senseless tragedy. As a member of the National Security Committee, I will work to make sure our security is strong within this country as well as strong outside our country.

However, one note of caution: During a senseless tragedy such as this, we must avoid recklessly affixing blame on people or groups who might be convenient targets for finger-pointing. This crime is being investigated by the appropriate law enforcement authorities and they will bring the perpetrators to justice.

We cannot allow the insanity of a few to become the justification for watering down the Bill of Rights. In short, we need to ensure that Washington-based elitists don't use this situation as pretext for declaring open season on those with opposing views or, God forbid, establishing a police state.

If we succumb to the fear, the bomber will have won. If we politicize the situation, the bomber will have won. If we abrogate our civil liberties and trample the Constitution, the bomber will have won. If we live with constant second-guessing and paranoia, the bomber will have won. If we allow people to label those with opposing views as hatemongers, the bomber wins. If we can't declare with resounding unanimity that this is still the greatest place in the world to live, the bomber will have won. We cannot allow the bomber to win.

Mr. Speaker, I have never been more proud to be an Oklahoman or an American, and I ask God with a prayerful heart to give this Congress and the president the wisdom and understanding to act responsibly and decisively in the coming weeks to do our best to ensure that this will never happen again.

The Grief Process

MOST PSYCHOTHERAPISTS AND OTHERS WHO work with persons who have suffered trauma and loss recognize five stages in the grieving process. Each step might last a few short moments or hang in for weeks. Every person differs.

There are two unhealthy situations: In one, the person refuses to work through the stages or for some reason cannot; in the other, the person gets stuck in one stage and cycles that one continually without moving on. Anger and depression, for example, are two stages which frequently mire people and retard healing.

1. Shock, disbelief. "Oh, [expletive of choice]!"; "This cannot have happened to me!"; "I don't believe it!"; "Oh, no!"

The initial reaction to the precipitating event, shock and disbelief, can be complicated by pain or physical injury. This is not the same shock to which medical people refer. *Traumatic shock* is a physiological result of sudden physical injury and has nothing to do with emotional or cognitive (thought-centered) shock.

2. Anger. Anger is never welcomed by friends and family, but it is a very important, necessary part of the process. Anger in children may express itself as acting out, weeping, screaming, violent reaction. Within reason (bashing baby brother with a bat is out), anger must be allowed, particularly in children.

3. Bargaining, conniving. "If You take care of this, God, I will be so good"; "Heal me, God, and I'll do such-and-so for You." (bargaining with the top man); "If I just change my ways and shape up, it will all come right." (bargaining with the self); "If an hour of therapy is good, two hours will be better." (conniving)

Bargaining and conniving are based neither in logic nor knowledge. They are conscious or unconscious attempts to manipulate God, humankind, and the self into changing reality. It is the lazy person's way out, so to speak, an end run around the hard work of recovery. Everyone goes through this stage to some degree.

4. Depression, sadness. This is the core of grieving and the stage most people recognize as actual grief. In reality, it is only one of the steps one must follow. It is usually the one that gets the most sympathy and understanding. People around the sufferer become very uncomfortable about putting up with the anger stage or the illogical nonsense of the bargaining stage, but they allow depression and sadness.

Be aware that depression can express itself in children as anger, acting out, volatility (explosiveness, moodiness), insomnia, and other surprising symptoms. If unexpected symptoms such as these occur in a child you know, suspect grief. Kids, incidentally, need not be directly involved in trauma. They can blot up fear and revulsion from others without themselves understanding the enormity of it.

5. Resignation, emergence. The shock has worn off. The bargaining didn't work. The anger and sadness cleansed. Now at last comes recovery. The victim resigns the self to reality and gets on with life.

For most people, there is no clear line defining this stage. Usually, the victim or survivor realizes one day that although the loss will always be there, the pain has subsided. This is the way life is.

The Irish said it well: *Life is meant to break your heart.*

N O T E S

Chapter Two

1. Maria Ruiz Scaperlanda, "Celebrating the Life of Valerie Koelsch," *The Sooner Catholic,* 4 June 1995.
2. Editorial, *Daily Oklahoman,* 20 April 1995.

Chapter Three

1. Jack Money, "Elevator Workers Played Rescue," *Daily Oklahoman,* 14 May 1995.
2. Cheryl Walker, "Trade Show Transformation," *Midsouthwest Restaurant Magazine,* May/June 1995, 10.

Chapter Four

1. Maria Ruiz Scaperlanda, "Celebrating the Life of Valerie Koelsch," *The Sooner Catholic,* 4 June 1995.
2. Poetry given with permission by Beverly Sumner.

Chapter Five

1. Jim Killackey, "Animals Cheer Saddened Kids," *Daily Oklahoman,* 25 April 1995.
2. Steve Lackmeyer, "July '94 Drill Foreshadowed," *Daily Oklahoman,* 23 April 1995.

Chapter Nine

1. See Deuteronomy 31:6.
2. Words and music © Anne Wilson, with permission.

Chapter Ten

1. Carla Hinton, *"Implosion Helps Lay Fears to Rest,"* *Daily Oklahoman,* 24 May 1995.

2. Karen Klinka, "Graduation Day Poignant Moment for Pamela Briggs," *Daily Oklahoman,* 13 May 1995.

3. Ellie Sutter, "Driver of UPS Delivery Truck Barely Escaped Blast," *Daily Oklahoman,* 1 May 1995.

4. Bobby Ross, Jr., and Bryan Painter, "Injured Fight to Rebuild After Bombing," *Daily Oklahoman,* 15 May 1995.

5. *Ibid.*

6. Carla Hinton, "Ruins Near School Become Chapel," *Daily Oklahoman,* 25 May 1995.

7. Jim Killackey, "Injured by Bomb, Survivor Worried" *Daily Oklahoman,* 3 June 1995.

Chapter Eleven

1. 2 Corinthians 11:14.

2. Matthew 27:46; Mark 15:34.

3. John 3:16.

4. Job 1:22.

5. See Job 2:3.

Chapter Twelve

1. Bob Stewart, "Answers to a Prayer," *People Magazine,* 15 May 1995, 106.

2. See 1 Corinthians 13:12.

3. Ecclesiastes 3:1–2.

Chapter Thirteen

1. Joe Hight, "Ongoing Effort for Rescuers," *Daily Oklahoman,* 8 May 1995.

2. Gypsy Hogan,"Yesterday I Just Kept Hugging Him," *Daily Oklahoman,* 21 April 1995.

Epilogue

1. The whippoorwill story is told in Max Lucado's *When God Whispers Your Name* (Dallas: Word, 1994). The

story of Sara can be found in Lucado's *A Gentle Thunder* (Dallas: Word, 1995).

Appendix C

1. Carla Hinton, "Boy's Past Time Cited in Blast Survival," *Daily Oklahoman,* 27 April 1995.
2. "Where They Died," *Daily Oklahoman,* 14 May 1995.
3. Ed Godfrey, "Mother of Spared Girl Mourns for Lost Children," *Daily Oklahoman,* 30 April 1995.